Morecambe and Lancaster

Harry Postlethwaite

© 2011 Venture Publications Ltd

ISBN 978 1905 304 424

CONTENTS

MORECAMBE, LANCASTER and the surrounding environs . . .

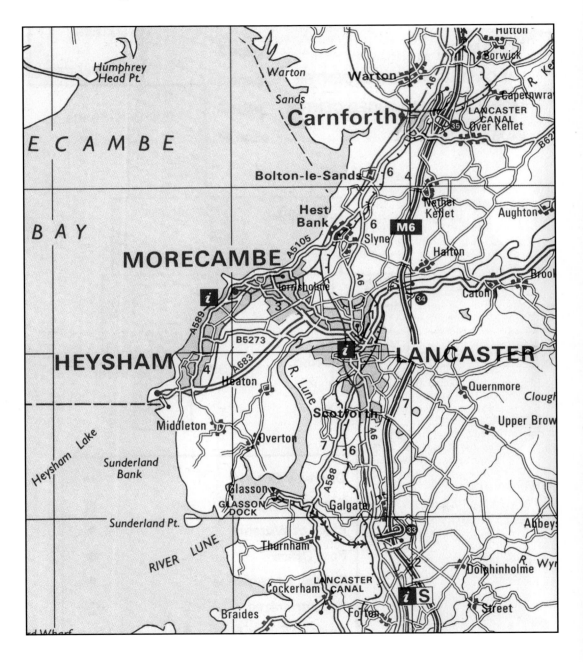

INTRODUCTION

The current boundaries of the City of Lancaster came into being under the Local Government Act 1972, becoming operational as from 1st April 1974. The area embraces five former local government districts, these being the municipal boroughs of Lancaster and Morecambe & Heysham, together with the Urban District of Carnforth and the Rural Districts of Lancaster and Lunesdale. The area forms the northern extremity of the County of Lancashire and comprises 222 square miles with a population of around 134,000.

The name was first recorded in the Domesday Book in 1086 as Loncastre and means 'Roman Fort on the River Lune'. It gained its first charter as a market town and borough in 1193 and was granted City status as late as 1937 for 'its long association with the Crown' and because it was 'the County Town of the King's Duchy of Lancaster'.

The Urban District Council of Morecambe and the Urban District Council of Heysham were established in 1894 and the Borough of Morecambe came into being on 24th June 1902 with the amalgamation of the villages of Poulton, Torrisholme and Bare. The Borough of Morecambe was combined with the Urban District of Heysham with effect from 1st October 1928 to form the Borough of Morecambe & Heysham.

Both Lancaster and Morecambe & Heysham had their own Transport Departments and these were combined following local government reorganisation in 1974. The story commences with early tramway operations and concludes with the takeover by Stagecoach in 1993.

The traditional boundaries of the Town/City of Lancaster straddled the A6 trunk road and this brought its problems with congestion over the years as traffic increased. These problems were greatly reduced with the opening, in April 1960, of the Lancaster bypass section of the M6 motorway. Even since this time traffic has further increased and brought congestion to the city centre, creating problems for transport operators attempting to operate services in accordance with a timetable.

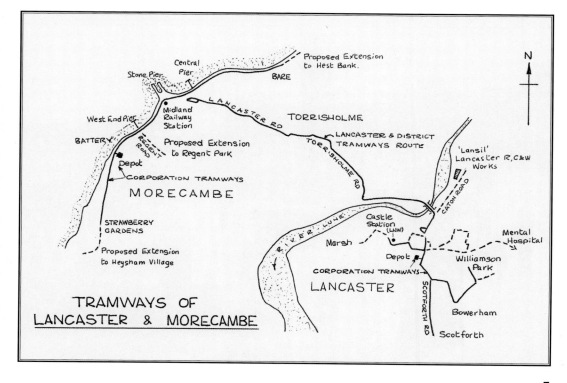

TRAMWAYS OF LANCASTER & MORECAMBE

TRAMWAYS
The 1870 Street Tramways Act

It was in 1870 that the Street Tramways Act became law and it had short term advantages for organisations seeking to develop tramways. However, it was not without its disadvantages for it required tramway operators to maintain the roadway between the tracks and also for a distance of 18 inches on both sides of the track. It also gave local authorities the absolute veto over the construction of tramways in their area and in addition, the power to take the tramway over after 21 years. All lines in this area were of standard gauge.

The Morecambe Tramways Company

On formation the company had four directors, Mr SJ Harris of Gillows and Company, Lancaster, Mr JT Marsden of S Thompson and Company, Lancaster, and Messrs E Gorrill and R Crabtree of Morecambe. A prospectus was issued in 1886 setting out the aims and objectives of the company and offering 1,600 shares of £10 each. The intention of the Company was to provide improved transport between Morecambe and Heysham for the benefit of visitors arriving by rail and for local residents. The Act materialised in 1886 as the Morecambe Tramways Act authorising the construction of two tramways.

The construction of the first of these tramways commenced in spring 1887 being 1¼ miles long from the new Central Pier to the Battery Hotel. The contractor for the construction was Mr Winnard of Wigan and the only difficulty encountered was that the road separating the jetty and the Midland Railway yard was crossed by 24 railway lines. A double line was provided from Central Pier to the centre of West View Terrace and a single line with two passing places from West View to the Battery. West View Terrace was between the junctions of Northumberland and Skipton Streets.

The original fleet comprised four horse-drawn tramcars, built by the Lancaster Carriage and Wagon Company, cars 1 and 2 being double-deck cars carrying 20 passengers inside and 24 outside. Cars 3 and 4 were open single-deck cars for summer use carrying 29 passengers. The original livery was maroon, teak and white.

An early scene at the Clock Tower on Morecambe's Central Promenade with horse-drawn trams very much in evidence. *(STA)*

The tramway was opened on Saturday 28th May 1887, following inspection on Wednesday 25th, with all four cars operating and filled to capacity, a total of 2,101 passengers being carried on this day. During this first year of operation the profit was £338 and at the Annual General Meeting a proposal was made for electrification but this was defeated, as it was when raised again in subsequent years. No Sunday service was provided initially.

The second phase of the line from the Battery to Strawberry Gardens, Heysham was opened on 19th May 1888, in readiness for the forthcoming season. Unlike phase one, which operated entirely on level ground, this tramway had to overcome Cross Cop, a hillock situated a few hundred yards on the Heysham side of the Battery. To overcome the problem of two horses struggling up the hill, a 'tip horse' was provided with a rider or 'tip lad' who was adept at attaching his horse's coupling to the side of the tram whilst it was moving in order to maintain the momentum. Once over the hill, the horse would await the tram travelling in the opposite direction. The line was single-track with four passing loops.

The numbers of passengers carried in the first three years of operation were:- 1887 – 253,560, 1888 - 495,222 and 1889 - 627,081. The associated profits were £338 9s 2d, £557 19s 4d and £999 12s 11d.

A further two cars numbered 5 and 6 were purchased in 1888, both being double-deck similar to numbers 1 and 2 and at a total cost of £373 10s 0d. A further single car No. 7 arrived in 1889. In 1890 the section from West View Terrace to the railway crossing was doubled and in July 1891 the section from the Battery to a point between Regent Road and Albert Road was reconstructed and doubled. Authorisation was granted under The Tramways Orders Confirmation Act 1892 for the construction of three further tramways and for the extension of Tramway No. 1. The tramways authorised were:-

Tramway No. 3 - 3 furlongs 5 chains in length from the open end of Tramway No. 1 to East View, which was the name of a house on the corner of Rossendale Avenue and was double-tracked throughout.

Tramway No. 4 – 6 furlongs 5 chains from the end of Tramway No. 3 along Bare Road to Bare. The terminus was to be the White House

A horse-drawn tram trundles along Morecambe Promenade with a full load of passengers. *(LCT)*

close to Elms Road junction. This tramway could not be built until the road was widened and had to be complete in three years otherwise the Parliamentary powers would expire.

Tramway No. 5 -1 furlong 8½ chains forming a junction with tramway No. 1 and then curving round along Regent Road to a point one chain away from the entrance to Regents Park.

Of these proposals, only Tramway No. 3 was built under this Order together with the additions to Tramway No. 1. On 17th June 1893 Tramway No. 3 from Central Pier to East View was opened and the Company-owned line was now at its maximum length of approximately three miles from Strawberry Gardens, Heysham to East View, Morecambe. Horse power was used throughout and the depot and stables were situated at Heysham Road opposite the Battery Inn on land later used as a bus park. It was relocated in 1897 to land which later became the site of Heysham Road Bus Depot. The boundary between Morecambe and Heysham crossed the system at the Battery Hotel.

By the time the original Confirmation Act 1892 expired, Tramway No. 4 had not been built but the Corporation then showed interest in the tramway and applied for Parliamentary Power which was received in the form of the Tramways Orders Confirmation No. 2 Act 1897. The arrangement was that the Council would build the tramway with operation by Morecambe Tramways Company. This section was built as single-track and following inspection on 26th April 1898 was opened on 23rd May 1898, four new double-deck cars of similar specification to the original ones being purchased at a cost of £150 each. The Company paid to the Corporation a fee of £150 per year for the lease of the tramway. Operation by the Company was on a ten year lease. There was a press item in July 1898 claiming that a 25-seat horse bus was running in competition between Central Pier and Bare but no further reference to this has been found.

In a resort such as Morecambe the seasonal changes in demand were significant and the Company dealt with this by selling most of its horses at the end of the season and buying more at the start of the new season. Additional similar cars, possibly second-hand numbered 12-15 arrived later with two more numbered 16 and 17 in 1901.

Above. With crowds in abundance a horse-drawn tram heads towards Bare along Morecambe Promenade, whilst in the distance another tram heads in the opposite direction. *(STA)*

Left. A lady passengers alights from tram number 8 at Bare on the last day of horse-drawn trams at Morecambe. *(LCT)*

After withdrawal car number 1 was sold to Manchester Corporation and used in a Civic procession in October 1926. Repainted in the red and white livery of the Manchester Carriage and Tramways Company, it is pictured outside Manchester's Car Works at Ardwick. *(STA)*

Morecambe Corporation Tramways

The tramway was attracting interest from outside parties including the British Tramway and Light Railway Association and a Mr George Balfour. It has been reported that at an extraordinary General Meeting of shareholders it was decided to sell to Mr Balfour but this decision was overturned by a meeting of Directors who objected to the tramway falling into the hands of a city holding company.

This aroused the interest of the Corporation and Articles of Agreement were signed on 29th November 1907 but this resulted in objections from the ratepayers. Mr Gardner, Manager of Transport Concerns for the City of Chester, was brought in to report. His recommendation was that the Corporation should take over the 1886 portion in accordance with the 1870 Tramways Act and compulsorily purchase by Act, the 1892 portion and arrange electrification of the whole length. Opposition from the ratepayers continued, fuelled by report of a loss made by the Lancaster and District Tramways Company and leading to a Public Meeting in the early part of 1908. At this meeting there was strong opposition to the

takeover which placed the Council in a difficult position. On 29th July 1908 it was announced that the Corporation had offered £7,661 for the system but the Company was asking £15,592. This resulted in deadlock and the matter went to arbitration and on 3rd February 1909 the arbitrators announced that they considered a price of £13,391 to be fair. Included in this price was the tramway from East View to the Battery, 12 cars, including two toastracks and a large part of Heysham Road depot, situated some 200 yards inside the Heysham boundary. Operating rights from the Battery terminus to the depot were arranged to between the Battery and Strawberry Gardens as this section was still owned by the Company. The deal was signed on 26th July 1909 and the first Corporation car operated on the same day. A party of Aldermen and Councillors travelled on the first tram from the Battery to Bare and back to the West View Hotel for light refreshments. Municipal transport in Morecambe had commenced. Some renumbering of the cars taken over seems to have occurred and two additional second-hand cars arrived quickly afterwards probably from the Morecambe Tramways Co. as replacements and leaving the Company with three cars.

During the winter of 1910/11 extensive work was carried out to double the track along large sections of the tramway with the cost being met in part by a grant of £12,225 from the Local Government Board. Pressure to electrify the system continued and in 1913 the *Tramway and Railway World* reported that the Corporation was considering the Edison-Beach accumulator system for their trams, presumably this being some form of battery operation to eliminate the need for overhead wiring. Four new replacement horse trams were purchased from English Electric Company in 1919 (Nos. 13 and 14) and 1922 (Nos. 15 and 16). Numbers 14 and 15 were 32-seat toastracks whilst 13 and 16 were double-deck. A fire occurred in the car sheds in June 1920, destroying the stables, the cars being rescued but the horses were not so lucky. The stables were rebuilt on the same site by 1922 and in that year a film was produced by the Samualson Film Co. The *Faithful Heart* which included tramway views between the Battery and the stables. Motor buses appeared in the fleet from 1919 but until 1922 merely duplicated the trams.

The pressure to electrify the system continued over the years but the change never came and Morecambe became the last town on mainland Britain to use horse-drawn trams which continued until the demise of the system in 1926. Latterly there were 12 cars operating and it was on 4th October 1926 that the last tram, No. 13, pulled by the two oldest horses, Adam and Eve, left the Battery at 8pm carrying passengers which included Alderman Hall, chairman of the Tramways Committee, the Mayor Alderman Gorton and the Editor of the *Morecambe Visitor*, Mr Gaunt. Alderman Hall drove the tram to Bare and the Mayor drove from Central Pier to the Battery. Speeches were made and testimony paid to the sterling service given by the trams. Horse car No. 1 was sold to Manchester Corporation for a civic procession, and then scrapped.

The Petrol Trams

Following the takeover of its assets within the Borough of Morecambe by the Corporation in 1909, the Company was left with the 1¼ mile line from the Battery to Strawberry Gardens, Heysham and three tramcars. Little is recorded of the Company activities over the next two years but there was, of course, capital in hand from the sale. This was used to purchase three petrol trams manufactured by Leyland Motors Ltd. These had Leyland petrol engines and single-deck bodies manufactured by the United Electric Car Company Ltd of Preston and lighting by Triers and Martin of London. In preparation for the coming of the petrol trams, the track was relaid between October 1911 and January 1912 using new 90lbs per yard rail in place of the original 65lbs per yard rail.

A ceremony was held on 15th January 1912 to mark the operation of the first petrol tram which was the first petrol traction tramcar to operate on public streets. The 'gaily decorated' car ran from the Battery to Bare and back through to Strawberry Gardens carrying a full load of invited dignitaries following which they lunched at the Grosvenor Hotel. The only reported drawback was meeting horse-drawn trams en-route and, of course, the tracks in Morecambe were not laid to the necessary standard for the additional weight of these cars. No further operation into Morecambe can be confirmed but may possibly have occurred. A fourth car of open layout was added in 1913.

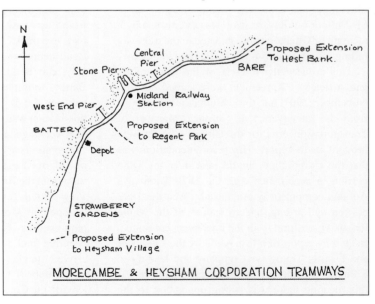

MORECAMBE & HEYSHAM CORPORATION TRAMWAYS

The service was successful with all four cars being in use during the summer season and with long queues forming at stops. During winter time the service was maintained with one car.

For a few months commencing March 1918, due to petrol shortage brought about by the first World War, the trams operated on town gas stored in large canvas containers with timber frame situated on the roof. The filling of the gas containers took place from the town gas supply which made the trams rather unpopular with domestic gas consumers who suffered gas shortage during

filling operations. Breakdowns became frequent and petrol operation had resumed by September when supplies were available. The engines were rated at 55hp mounted centrally with radiators and controls at each end of the car. The maximum speed was 12mph and petrol consumption of the order of eight miles per gallon. The takeover by the Corporation left the Company without accommodation for its tramcars and accordingly, an old timber horse bus shed was acquired and this was erected adjacent the Corporation depot to accommodate the fleet.

Above. A side elevation of one of Heysham's petrol-driven tramcars photographed when new. These were the first such cars to enter service in the country. *(LCT)*

Below. A scene celebrating the entry into service of the new cars. *(STA)*

In the postwar period a number of small bus operators emerged and the first to compete with trams was a Mr Jenkinson who bought two ex-London Tilling buses for operation along the tram route, commencing in February 1923, at a time when the trams were disadvantaged by having to terminate at Four Lane Ends, half a mile short of Strawberry Gardens due to track re-alignment work. The buses had the advantage that they could operate into the village of Heysham. In March 1923 the tramway company commenced bus operation, to counter this competition, using an ex-Ribble Karrier bus CK 3087.

The Morecambe Tramways Company continued its bus interests and signed an Agreement with Morecambe Corporation in 1924 to cover the operation of a bus service between Morecambe and Heysham. This started on 1st April 1924 from Bare to Heysham.

The petrol trams continued to operate after the advent of the buses but finally ceased operation on 24th October 1924 at the end of the summer season. The departure went unmarked and the trams were broken up for scrap by TW Ward of Sheffield who were ship breakers on the jetty. One car body passed to Heysham Golf Club as a Pro's workshop. Heysham UDC purchased all the lines in their district on 28th July 1924 to make way for road improvements. Access for the Corporation horse trams between the Battery and the depot had, of course, to be maintained.

The incorporation of the company Heysham and District Motors Ltd took place on 13th December 1924 with the main shareholders being Messrs Wright, Carr, Booth and Sykes of the Tramway Company together with Mr Hollings, a local motor engineer who later became General Manager. The intention of the new company was to carry on the bus operations of Morecambe Tramways Company and this had taken place by February 1925. The Morecambe Tramways Company remained in existence in order to complete the disposal of the tramway assets which passed to Heysham UDC on 17th February 1926.

On 23rd November 1926 a letter was sent to shareholders proposing to sell to Heysham Urban District Council on the grounds that 'competition in road transport is very keen, notwithstanding the bad state of trade during the past year and conditions are so precarious'. However, the takeover did not take place until 4th May 1929, after the merger of the Borough of Morecambe and Heysham Urban District Council.

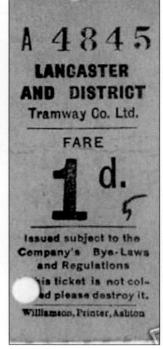

Above. A Lancaster and District Tramways horse-drawn tram arrives at the Lancaster terminus.

Right. A penny ticket as issued by the Lancaster and District Tramways Company. *(RA)*

The Lancaster and District Tramways Company

This part of the story commences in 1888 when the Lancaster and District Tramways Company was formed with the intention of applying to the Board of Trade for authorisation to operate a tramway. A prospectus was issued in 1889 and the directors were :- T Preston, Mayor of Lancaster and Director of Lancaster Banking Company, IH Storey, a well known local manufacturer, CJ Clarke of Cross Hill, W Hall, MD of Lancaster, JW Pickard and J Turney. In the prospectus it was claimed that the tramway would serve a population of 46,000. The initial capital was to be £20,000 in £1 shares with the eventual aim of £40,000. The prospectus stated that the intention was to use horse power initially, while powers were obtained to electrify the line. To enable the company to construct the second stage of the tramway from Stonewell to Scotforth, the Council had agreed to construct a road linking South Road and Thurnham Street through Prince William Henry Field and to widen Penny Street bridge. In addition to carrying passengers, the company intended to carry parcels and light goods. The revenue was estimated to be of the order of £7,000 per annum.

Although there was authorisation for the construction of a tramway from Morecambe to Scotforth, due to financial restrictions, only the portion from Morecambe to Stonewell was constructed. The appointed contractor was Mr Goldsworthy of St Helens and work commenced in January 1890. By 1st March The *Lancaster Guardian* was able to report that the first mile of track, at the Morecambe end, had been laid and much preparation had been carried out for the next section. On completion Major General Hutchinson RE, of the Board of Trade, arrived on Saturday 2nd August 1890 to carry out the inspection. Tram No. 1 left the depot at 11am with Major General Hutchinson, Alderman Preston, the Borough Surveyor and several other people walking at the rear. Trouble soon arose in that the tram derailed at the first corner turning out of Cable Street but this was soon remedied and the inspection was completed in about two hours. The party returned to the assembled crowd in Lancaster and after making several recommendations, Major General Hutchinson granted the Company a licence to operate for a six months trial period. The route

between the two towns lay along what were the only suitable roads, through Torrisholme and Scale Hall and then over Skerton Bridge.

Many of those who had gathered were keen to try out the new system and No. 1 left the depot at 3pm with a full load on its first revenue earning journey. Around 1,600 passengers were carried on this first day of operation. There were further problems over the next few days with one tram on the Sunday being derailed four times and taking 1¼ hours to complete the journey. On the Monday, one tram suffered a broken rear axle which had to be repaired at the Carriage and Wagon Works on Caton Road but after these initial problems, the tramway operated relatively smoothly.

Objections came from the Stonewell area of Lancaster regarding the noise and disturbance caused by the trams and the horses on Sunday with the objectors pointing out that the Morecambe trams did not operate on Sundays 'in deference to the Sabbath'. The Company compromised by using a point opposite the Yorkshire House in Parliament Street as the Lancaster terminal point on Sundays.

The length of the line was 4 miles 2 furlongs 4 chains and 30 links mainly single-track with passing loops and a loop at each end. The Morecambe terminus was near the old Royalty Theatre on Market Street with the two sides of the loop running along Euston Road and Cheapside. At the end of the loop, the line ran parallel to the Morecambe tramway but there was no connection between the two. At the Lancaster end the tracks along Cable Street, North Road and Chapel Street formed a triangle, the lines from North Road and Chapel Street running parallel from the junction of the roads to meet at Stonewell. Originally the tramway offices were at Stonewell, opposite the points, but were moved in the early part of the 20th century from the building which is now the Post Office to 114 St Leonardgate. The section over Cross Hill required a 'trace horse' similar to that described for the Morecambe Tramway at Cross Cop.

A local guide book for 1891 praised the tramway with the wording:-

'The journey between Morecambe and Lancaster by tram is simply charming and health giving. Great praise is due to L&D Tramways Co. Ltd for the foresight and determination they have displayed in projecting and carrying out their

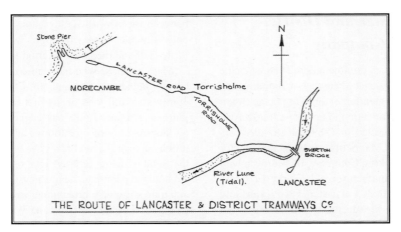

THE ROUTE OF LANCASTER & DISTRICT TRAMWAYS Cº

tramways. Grave difficulties met them at every step & many obstacles which seemed insuperable had to be overcome. Pluck and determination prevailed.'

The journey time between Lancaster and Morecambe by tram in 1911 was 35 minutes with a fare of 4d. This compared with 15 minutes by train with a fare of 3d. A timetable for June 1908 show weekday frequencies of 20 minutes and evenings 30 minutes, from 8.20am ex-Morecambe until 10.30pm ex-Lancaster. An early morning workmens' car also operated. The Sunday service started from Morecambe at 11.50am and operated 'every few minutes' until 10.45pm ex-Lancaster.

The cars were 14 fairly standard open-top double-deckers of the time built by Lancaster Carriage and Wagon Company. Some of these were later altered to single-deck open cars by lowering the top deck to car waist level. The double-deckers were hauled by 3 horses and due to the seasonal nature of the business, a horse sale was held at the end of each season. The sale took place in the yard of the County Hotel and the 1895 catalogue stated that 85 horses were for sale, only 12 being retained.

The main depot and stables was situated at Lancaster Road, Morecambe on a site which was later occupied by Ribble Motor Services Ltd as their Morecambe depot. At Lancaster the Company had an arrangement with a local garage owner which allowed them to park one or two cars on this site. It is recorded that in 1895 the Lancaster drivers were paid 25s per week and the conductors 23s per week after a starting wage of 21s per week. During the winter period the drivers' wage dropped to 21s per week but the stablemen received 22s 6d for a seven day week throughout the year.

The Company extended its operations from February 1908 by trying a horse bus from Lancaster Market Square to Skerton. The experiment ceased after 16 weeks, a profit of only £5 having been made over the period. The Company did, at one time, operate a number of horse drawn road vehicles, one of these being an old coach which was used to provide excursions to the Lune Valley and Kirkby Lonsdale.

Profitability became poor and although horse traction was becoming outdated, there were insufficient funds available to allow the Company to consider electrification. This situation was not helped by the beginning of the First World War in 1914. In April 1914 the Company introduced two, soon to be increased to four, motor buses which were the first to operate in the area but the chassis were commandeered for War Service in September. These had been supplied by arrangement with Fahy's Ltd, the local Leyland dealer and charabanc proprietor trading as 'Royal Red'. Wartime restraints following the commandeering of horses also reduced the car service by October 1914 to a 45 minute frequency with 30 minutes at weekends. In January 1915 an Agreement was reached with Fahy's Ltd and buses were reintroduced. The new operation was a joint bus committee of Lancaster and District Tramways Company and Fahy's Ltd, each having a 50% share in vehicle ownership and profits. The trams remained outside this arrangement.

After this, the tram service was limited to a few journeys daily, using one car to keep the Company's rights intact, and ceased operation on New Year's Eve, 1921. One eye witness recalled:-

"The trams were built to carry 40 but there can't have been less than 140 folk on't last 'un."

A fitting epitaph to the last Lancaster and District tram appeared in a piece, in a local paper, describing the departure of the last tram from Morecambe on a Saturday night-

'The tram with its full complement of passengers would then slowly pull away with its wheel flanges and horses' steel shod hooves grinding sparks from the track. The noise of its progress and the clatter of the horses' hooves on the stone setts would gradually die away as the last faint glimmerings of the oil lamps flickered to extinction in the distance. The last tram had gone.'

In 1921 the Company had approached Lancaster Council in an attempt to sell their assets and the tracks were sold to the Lancaster and Morecambe Councils to allow road improvements. The Lancaster and District Tramways Company and Fahy's Ltd joint bus arrangement continued to develop services in the area until it was amalgamated with other operators into the new BAT subsidiary Lancashire and Westmorland Motor Services in February 1926.

Lancaster Corporation Tramways

In May and June 1899 both the Knott End Railway and the Fleetwood and Morecambe Light Railway made application to the Lancaster Borough Council to bring light railways into the area. The Council objected to this and formed a sub-committee to further the objection to these proposals and to investigate the provision of a scheme of their own. The first light railway proposal was tabled at a Council meeting on 8th May 1899 with a second proposal being tabled on 16th June 1899. On the basis of this second proposal, the Borough Surveyor was instructed to prepare a scheme for a possible tramway network.

The Council was already presenting to Parliament in 1900 a Bill authorising various works within the Borough and application for tramway powers could be added to this Bill at minimal expense. Between June and November 1899 the Borough Surveyor inspected various tramway systems and used the knowledge gained to prepare a system for Lancaster, plans for which were tabled at a council meeting on 6th November 1899. A route mileage of 8 miles 7 furlongs was proposed of which 1 mile 5 furlongs would be double-tracked. All districts of the Borough were to be covered with the exception of Skerton to the north which was considered to be covered by the Lancaster and District Tramway Company. The estimated

cost was £70,000 including the purchase of the Lancaster and District system. A meeting of the Tramways Committee also took place on 6th November and was attended by Mr Allan Sewart of the County Asylum Visiting Committee, later renamed Moor Hospital, who requested that the line linking the asylum to the London and North Western Railway Station be arranged to carry coal and other heavy traffic in railway wagons. To meet with this request, the Town Clerk was instructed to insert a clause within the Bill to cover the 'asylum goods line'. The surveyor estimated that if lines 9, 10, 11, 12 and 13 were constructed to carry goods traffic, the cost would be £79,464 compared to £74,057 without this facility.

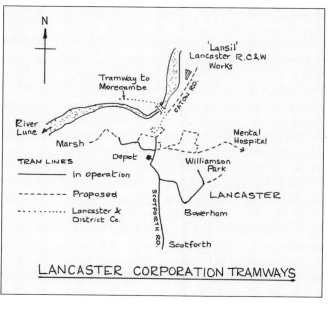

LANCASTER CORPORATION TRAMWAYS

A long and protracted wrangle began with the Lancaster and District Tramways Company in early 1900 regarding the takeover by the Council of the system. This wrangle carried over into the days of Ribble Motor Services Ltd, with regard to the operation by Ribble of services between Lancaster and Morecambe. On 17th February 1900 Lancaster and Morecambe Councils met and agreed an offer for the takeover of the Tramways Company.

Objections to the Tramway Bill were raised by London & North Western Railway Company, the Lancaster Asylums Board and the Lancaster Billposting Company. These were dealt with independently and successfully. On learning of the discouraging results of the Lancaster and District Tramways Company shareholders meeting, the Town Council dropped from the Bill the clause relating to the Company. Estimates for carrying goods to the asylum were declared as follows:-

4,000 – 6,000 tons 2/3d per ton
6,000 – 8,000 tons 2/- per ton
over 8,000 tons 1/9d per ton

A letter dated 3rd May from Mr Sewart declared that these rates were completely unacceptable to the Asylum Visiting Committee and the matter did not proceed further.

The Lancaster Corporation Act, including clauses relating to the tramway, was finalised on 6th August 1900. The post of Tramways and Electrical Engineer was advertised at a salary of £300 per annum and 34 applications were received. The successful applicant was Mr Tester of Plymouth who commenced his duties on 2nd March 1901. During the first half of 1901 a Birmingham syndicate led by a Mr WJ Kershaw, a chartered accountant, expressed an interest in purchasing the Corporation tramway rights and the Lancaster and District tramway company with a view to electrifying the latter. The Corporation was not interested and nothing further came of it.

One of Mr Tester's first jobs was to prepare an estimate of cost for the first two lines and a figure of £25,966 was provided for the lines from Dalton Square to Bowerham and Scotforth with a further estimate of £1,325 for the provision of a new tram shed to be built off Nelson Street, at the south-east corner of Dalton Square, next to the planned new Town Hall. These figures were approved by the Council on 26th June with a resolution to carry on. Contracts were then let for the various sections of work as follows:-

Section A	Rails, fishplates etc., Messrs Walter Scott Ltd, Leeds.	
Section B	Platelaying, Mr Ernest Ireland, Morecambe.	
Section C	Overhead Equipment, Messrs Lowden Brothers & Co., Dundee	
Section D	Feed Cables, Pilot Wires etc., Callendar Cables Construction Co,. London.	
Section E	Tram Cars, British Westinghouse Manufacturing Co. Ltd. Subject to bodies being by Lancaster Carriage and Wagon Co.	

On 18th November 1902 current was switched on for the two lines to Bowerham and Scotforth to allow testing to take place and interviewing for drivers and conductors took place two days later. Initially, ten double-deck cars built on the reverse staircase principle were delivered with accommodation for 18 passengers inside and 24 outside. They were mounted on Brill trucks with a 6ft wheelbase, this being slightly shorter than standard in order to meet local conditions. They were powered by 25hp motors with a controller of the series parallel type with brake notches and connections for Westinghouse brakes in case of emergency. The livery was chocolate and primrose with the corporation arms.

The tram shed was large enough to accommodate 20 trams and the track was laid to a gauge of 4ft. 8½ins, with a gap of 4ft between the rails for double-track sections. On 16th December 1902 the Council instructed the Tramway Engineer to produce an estimate for a further line from Dalton Square to Willow Lane which would serve Lancaster Castle Railway Station.

On 6th January 1903 Board of Trade inspectors, Lt Colonel Yorke and Mr Trotter arrived to inspect the track and electrical aspects and permission to open the tramway was received by telegraph on Tuesday 13th January 1903. Included in the recommendation that came with permission was one that the track at Bowerham Hill should be doubled. The tramways sub-committee responded quickly to this and arrangements were made for an official

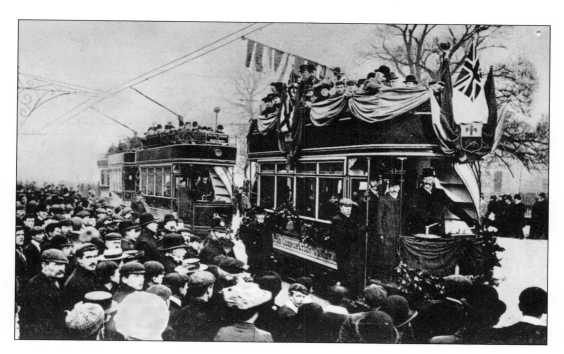

Upper. Scenes of great celebration on Wednesday 14th January 1903 with the opening of the Lancaster Corporation electric tramway system. Tram number 1 is appropriately at the head of the procession .*(LCT)*

Right. Tram number 3, now with top cover, arrives at Scotforth with motorman Bill Gates at the controls. *(HPC)*

opening ceremony the following day. The invited guests included members of the Borough Council, officials of concerns with tramway interests and members of the press. The *Lancaster Guardian* reported that it had aroused more interest than any other recent local event.

The ceremony commenced at 1.30pm with a tour of the depot followed by a tour of the system in three trams led by No. 1 suitably decorated for the occasion and driven by the Mayor, Alderman George Jackson, under the supervision of Mr Tester. The journey from Dalton Square to the terminus at Scotforth took nine minutes with small crowds gathered along the track side. After returning to the Pointer, the trams carried the guests along the Bowerham route to Williamson Park Gates. On arriving back at the Town Hall the guests were entertained to a luncheon with the Mayor. In speaking of the construction of the tramway, Alderman Smith commented 'their engineer had not gone very fast, but he had been very sure. He had not got on as fast perhaps as energetic northern people would have liked.' In his own speech, Mr Tester the engineer replied that he could not agree that there had been any great delay in the construction of the tramway. He had been in the hands of northern contractors,

whereas he had been used to southern contractors who moved much faster.

The fares were arranged in halfpenny stages with aggregate fares for the whole route. The *Lancaster Guardian* reported that the first passengers found the 'breeze from Clougha Pike exceptionally keen as the last two halfpenny stages were entered upon.' Altogether 3,033 passengers travelled on the first day and regular operation commenced the following day at 7am. The following Monday, reduced fare workmens cars started operating.

On 3rd April 1903 Mr Tester reported back to the Council on the proposed additional tram route and offered two alternatives. The one chosen was from Dalton Square via Market Street, Common Garden Street, King Street, Meeting House Lane to terminate in Station Road. Doubling of the track on the Bowerham route to meet the recommendations of the Board of Trade took place in 1903 but did not completely remove the dangers of this area. The steep hill combined with a sharp bend and trees lining the road caused problems in wet weather when the trees were losing their leaves and several runaways did leave the track at the points on South Road. It seems that 'leaves on the line' reported in recent years in connection

The system was extended to serve Castle Railway Station and tram number 11 displays this destination in the window when photographed with its crew looking very proud of their tram. *(LCT)*

with railways were not a new phenomenon. Further doubling of the track from the Pointer to Thurnham Street was authorised later in the year.

The first year's operation was financially not good with a loss of £2,833 being recorded, a high figure for a tramway at that time.

The new line serving Castle Railway Station was inspected in September 1904 and the line opened the following month. The Williamson Park service was soon reduced to operate to the Park only at popular visiting times, terminating at Bowerham (Coulston Road) at other times. In 1905 the depot was relocated from the old site near Dalton Square towards the south end of Thurnham Street over to the west side, the old site being used for the new Town Hall Gardens. The opening of the new route necessitated the purchase of two additional trams, which arrived in 1905, and these were provided with Milnes-Voss bodies which were cheaper than bodies by the local firm Lancaster Carriage and Wagon Company. They featured direct staircases and Mountain and Gibson trucks.

For a short period from 1905 to 1908 through tickets were available in conjunction with London and North Western Railway Company, from Morecambe to Lancaster and then on to Williamson Park using the trams. This was discontinued following a decision at the Council meeting in May 1908.

In every year between 1903 and 1910 the tramway made a loss, the worst year being 1905 when an operating loss of £732 was recorded. It may have been this loss which initiated interest in the operation of motor buses and in 1905 members of the Tramways Sub-Committee visited the Automobile Show in London but nothing further came of this at that time. Concern was expressed over the running of open-top trams and a delegation visited Bolton and Preston, coming back with a favourable report on the Bolton top covers which was presented to the Council Meeting on 7th February 1911. Arising from this four covers were ordered from Milnes-Voss and after fitting, a further two were ordered. Two further conversions took place in 1913, this time by United Electric Car Company of Preston, Milnes-Voss being unable to complete this order. Four cars, however, remained open-topped.

Tram number 12 stands outside the entrance to Williamson Park with its crew ready for the return journey. *(LCT)*

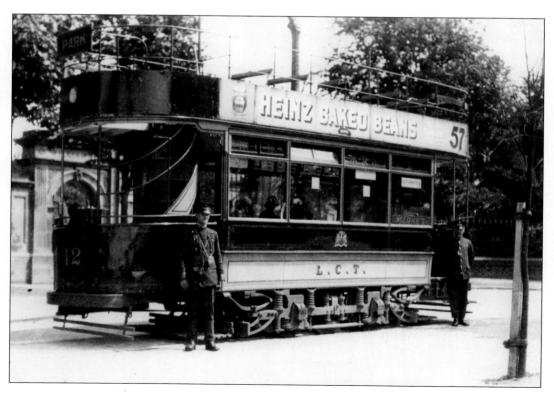

There were concerns that, although the tramway system only covered parts of the town, the whole town was subsidising it. The First World War started and a munitions works was established on Caton Road and the workers required transport. To meet this demand, the Council ordered three US-built Edison-electric omnibuses and the first two to arrive were put to work on a service to Skerton on 30th November and they were joined by a third such vehicle in January 1917 for the service to the munitions works. The 22-seat bodies were by Brush of Loughborough and each bus had a set of batteries which were charged from a generator in Market Square, the base from which the buses operated. The main problem with them was that they struggled on even a slight gradient which meant that their use in Lancaster was severely restricted and so was confined to the Caton Road and Skerton services. Two more were added in 1918 bodied by a local firm and were unusual in having entrances on the vehicle front. These enabled a new service to Marsh to begin. The Caton Road service finished by 1921 and a new service to Freehold was started soon afterwards. Bearing in mind the life expectancy of early buses, the battery operated fleet remarkably remained in service until 1929.

To revert to the trams, they continued to be unprofitable and some were showing signs of their age. The double-deckers became notorious for running away on the slope of Bowerham Hill resulting in several fatalities and it was decided to convert some of the cars to single-deckers. The first car to be converted was number 11, late in 1917, and after removal of the top-deck vestibule ends were fitted and it became known as the 'coffin car'. It was arranged for one-man-operation and the cost of the conversion was £40. At a Council Meeting on 29th April 1919 it was agreed to convert further double-deck cars to single-deck and by July 1920 six cars had been converted. On 10th July 1920 the Market Entrance to Castle Station route was closed, it having been previously reported that the track was in poor condition. The route was also covered by the existing Marsh bus route. The other tram routes now used the Market Entrance rather than Dalton Square as a terminus. In 1921 the Lancaster and District Company approached Lancaster and Morecambe Corporations, offering to sell their assets for £4,000 but nothing came of this, as previously reported. The year 1922 saw the lifting of the Castle Station and the Lancaster and District lines.

The first Lancaster Corporation petrol driven bus arrived in 1925 and this really signalled the end of the road for the tramways. In September 1928 it was decided that the Bowerham and Scotforth tram routes should be withdrawn but the trams continued to operate into the next decade. However, the end for the Bowerham route came on 18th January 1930 when tram number 10 left the Market Entrance at 11.15pm with Charlie Williams, conductor on the first tram, as driver. On reaching Bowerham, Alderman Curwen, chairman of the Tramways Sub-Committee made an impromptu speech and outside the Bowerham Hotel, crowds gathered and sang 'Auld lang syne.'

The end for the Scotforth route came on 31st March 1930 with the system's last three double-deckers all taking part. Number 8 was decorated for the occasion and used to convey invited guests. The driver was Alderman George Jackson, driver of the first tram, and Alderman Curwen was the conductor with Driver Charlie Williams supervising the amateur crew. The last tram, carrying the slogan 'The Old gives way to the New - 1903-1930' left the Market Entrance at 4pm and on arrival at Scotforth terminus, speeches were made, the first being by Alderman Jackson, who remarked on the fine workmanship of the Lancaster Carriage and Wagon Company. It was stated that the tramway had served the town well having carried 38,590,969 passengers and travelled 4,290,323 miles.

The trams returned to the depot at 4.45pm when Alderman Jackson applied the magnetic brake rather harshly resulting in a comment from the 'conductor' "Mr Mayor, pay that driver off when we return to the depot". The troubles on Lancaster's trams continued to the end with the second car coming to a halt on the curve into the depot and having to be manhandled the last few yards.

An era in Lancaster's transport history had ended, the trams had gone and from now on, buses were to reign supreme.

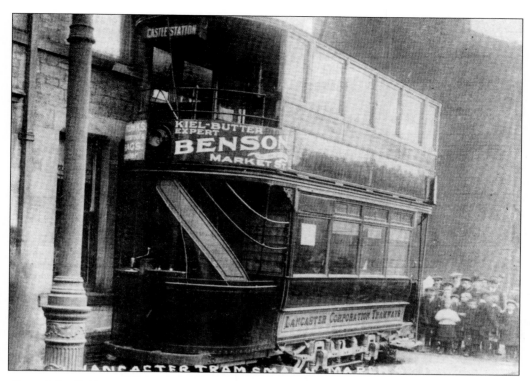

Above. A derailed tram can be guaranteed to attract attention, particularly from children as illustrated by this picture of tram number 7 derailed en route to Castle Railway Station on 4th March 1912. *(LCT)*

Below. 31st March 1930 was the final day of tramway operation with a well loaded unidentified car suitably decorated for the occasion. *(LCT)*

LANCASTER CORPORATION
Early Buses

As reported in the previous chapter, Lancaster Corporation's first experience of bus operation came about in 1916 when the first two of an order for three Brush-bodied 22-seat Edison battery-electric buses were put into service. Another two arrived in 1918 which differed from the first three in having locally built 25-seat bodies of unique design. Although said to be poor on gradients, all five vehicles lasted until 1929 when they were sold to Leeds Hygienic Laundry, most likely for their battery equipment.

Under the Lancaster Order 1916 bus services were confined to the Borough and this continued until 1931 when an amendment removed this restriction.

After 1918, no further buses were purchased until 1925 when the first petrol engined bus arrived. It was a Daimler CKA with 24-seat body by Buckingham and was followed at the end of the year by a 14-seat Overland BMT with body by local coachbuilder Barton Townley. Both vehicles and all subsequent deliveries had pneumatic tyres from new.

A 32-seat Buckingham-bodied Daimler CM arrived in 1926, followed in 1927 by a 24-seat Buckingham-bodied Daimler CKA. An ADC 424 model with body by G Fox, believed to have been subcontracted from local bodybuilder Barton Townley, arrived in 1928 and was the only ADC ever operated by Lancaster. The first Leylands arrived in 1928 being Lioness models with Leyland 26-seat bodies and they were joined by a further example in 1929. These three were to remain the only Leylands in the fleet during the prewar period. The year 1929 also saw a return to Daimler as chassis supplier, a make which was to predominate in the Lancaster fleet for some years to come. These three examples, together with eight which followed in 1930, were of the CF6 model and introduced a new supplier of bodywork in that they were fitted with 26-seat bodies by Northern Counties Motor and Engineering Company of Wigan. Lancaster was unusual among municipal

Lancaster Bus Station was a scene familiar to many travellers, not just those local, but also on inter-urban services and long distance services to the Lake District, Scotland and Yorkshire. This scene dating from June 1957 shows a mixture of Lancaster Corporation and Ribble buses. *(KS)*

Above. Edison battery-powered bus number 1 stands in Market Square, connected to the battery charging point for its return journey to the Caton Road projectile factory. *(LCT)*

Below. 1926 Daimler number 8 (TD 4921), with Buckingham body, awaits departure from Market Square with a battery-powered bus to the right and an unidentified vehicle behind. *(LCT)*

Above. Photographed when new in 1932 is number 23 (TF 9646), an AEC Regent with body by English Electric. Lancaster's first double-decker, it was renumbered 5 in 1934. The body was reconditioned by East Lancashire Coachbuilders in 1942 and it was withdrawn in 1945. (LCT)

Upper left. The first of many Daimler COG5 models to enter the fleet arrived in 1936 and were fitted with English Electric bodies. All remained in service until 1952-54 and ATF 556, originally numbered 6, is shown in service in May 1952. (RM)

Lower left. A posed photograph of number 26 (ATF 558), a Daimler COG5 with body by English Electric, when new in 1936. (LCT)

operators in preferring normal-control single-deck vehicles up to and including the 1930 supplies.

The arrival of new vehicles in 1929 had enabled the operator to withdraw the battery-operated vehicles with which bus operation had commenced in 1916. Considering the comments which had been made about the battery-operated vehicles, particularly with regard to limited hill climbing ability and the need for frequent recharging of the batteries, they had remarkably long lives with the operator. The vehicles supplied in 1930 were needed for tram replacement services following the cessation of the trams.

A similar ex-demonstrator Daimler CF6 with 26-seat Northern Counties body was acquired in February 1931 and was followed later in the year by the first heavyweight single-decker, a Daimler CH6 model with Weymann body. Lancaster was late in joining the ranks of double-deck operators with the result that it never operated open staircase types or that doyen of double-deckers of the late twenties and early thirties, the piano-fronted Leyland Titan, although there were many examples of this type operating in the area in the fleet of Ribble Motor Services.

In 1931 two Daimler CF6 single-deckers, one with Buckingham and one with Northern Counties body, were operated on hire from Daimler Limited, Coventry. Unlike previous CF6 models they were of forward-control layout, enabling seating capacity to be increased to 32 and were subsequently acquired in early 1932.

Their size required the employment of conductors again but one-person-operation of 26-seaters continued until 1940 after which conductors had to be used. Also acquired, in September 1932, was an ex-demonstrator Daimler CP6 double-decker with Burlingham body. It was modified to CH6 by 1937, probably using the engine from a withdrawn CF6, in order to standardise with other petrol units in the fleet. The body was overhauled by Massey Brothers, Wigan in March 1938 but twelve months later it was damaged in an accident with a low bridge and subsequently repaired by Burlingham, after which it remained in the fleet until September 1943. Quite a chequered history.

Following the lifting of restrictions on operating outside the boundary, a new service was tried to rural Aldcliffe in 1932 but this did not last long.

Interest in double-deckers was obviously growing and a further demonstrator was operated on loan in October 1932. This was an AEC Regent, registered MV 1518, with Brush body which had been new in February 1932 and it was subsequently acquired in November 1932 through Tillotson, a dealer in Burnley. In addition, a new AEC Regent, registered TF 9646, with English Electric body was purchased through Tillotson in November 1932. Both AEC Regents received 7.7 litre AEC diesel engines in March 1935.

Prior to July 1935 a standard fare of 1½d was charged but this was considered by some to be too high and from this time fares were charged at 1d per mile. In the same month route numbers were introduced.

The double-deck fleet was further expanded in 1934 when two further double-deckers were purchased. These introduced a new make to the fleet in that they were Crossley Condors with Crossley bodies and were the first vehicles in the fleet to be fitted with diesel engines. Another event of 1934 was the complete renumbering of the fleet. The year 1936 saw the arrival in the fleet of the Daimler COG5 chassis with five cylinder Gardner engine, a chassis type which was to be standard for Lancaster up to and including the year 1940, after which deliveries were determined in accordance with wartime restrictions as detailed later.

Both single- and double-deck examples of this chassis were purchased as detailed in the fleet summary, all the bodies in the years 1936 to 1938 inclusive being by English Electric Company.

A significant milestone in the history of Lancaster was reached in 1937 when it was granted city status for 'its long association with the Crown' and because it was 'the county town of the King's Duchy of Lancaster'. Accordingly, the name of the transport undertaking was changed from *Lancaster Corporation Transport* to *Lancaster City Transport*. In July 1937 the new garage and office building was opened in Kingsway.

The year 1939 was significant for a number of reasons. In February three new Daimler COG5 models arrived, two with single-deck and one with double-deck bodies, all by Willowbrook of Loughborough, a new make for Lancaster. The new Damside Street Bus Station was opened jointly with Ribble Motor Services on 1st April and thereafter, all services entering the City

Centre were routed via the Bus Station, the main Corporation loading point having previously been Market Square. On the same date an interesting but short-lived co-ordinated service was introduced, following pressure from the traffic commissioners. Lancaster worked jointly with Ribble between Scotforth (Boot and Shoe) and Morecambe (Euston Road) and Ribble picked up local passengers for the first time on their trunk services south of the city. The former Scotforth tram replacement service was withdrawn as a result of this operation. However, following the outbreak of World War 2 in September 1939, services reverted to the earlier arrangement. One of the main reasons cited was the problem of outbound local passengers crowding trunk passengers off the Ribble services.

Wartime

The war was to have a major effect on the operators of transport services for several years to come with regard to fuel restrictions and the supply of new vehicles. The fuel restrictions applied almost immediately and Lancaster introduced a revised timetable which took effect from Saturday 16th September 1939.

A further timetable was introduced with effect from 11th August 1940 and was surprisingly issued in the form of a booklet. Many operators at this time used folded sheets for timetables in the knowledge that there would be further revisions in the near future as the fuel situation either worsened or eased. The restrictions on the supply of new vehicles took longer to emerge. Initially, operators were able to take delivery of vehicles already on order and in January 1940 a further three Daimler COG5 models arrived. As with the 1939 delivery, there were two single-deck and one double-deck bodies, all by Willowbrook. An unusual delivery in 1941 was of a TSM H5LA4 model with 26-seat single-deck body by Willowbrook. It had originally been intended for China Omnibus Company and was no doubt diverted due to wartime restrictions. It had perimeter seating and had a short life with Lancaster, being sold to Trimdon Motor Services, Trimdon, County Durham in March 1945.

Restrictions were placed on the manufacture of buses and stocks of materials held by manufacturers were 'frozen', the intention being that manufacturers would divert their production facilities to the war effort. It was then realised that buses would be required to transport workers in connection with the war effort and the stocks previously 'frozen' were then 'unfrozen' and manufacturers were allowed to build vehicles from these stocks. These vehicles were referred to as 'unfrozen vehicles' and they were allocated to operators on the basis of need, no account being taken of operators preferences for manufacturer. Under this scheme, Lancaster received one Leyland TD7 double-decker with body by East Lancashire Coachbuilders of Blackburn. It was further realised that the number of vehicles which could be manufactured from unfrozen stocks would be inadequate to meet the need of operators. As a result of this conclusion, a specification for a utility chassis and body was drawn up by the Ministry of War Transport in conjunction with the National Association of Vehicle Body Builders and an order to build an initial batch of 500 was placed with Guy Motors of Wolverhampton for the chassis and a number of coachbuilders were authorised to build the bodies. The Guy chassis can best be described as 'simple but rugged' and the bodies as a 'no frills' design with lack of interior lining panels, lack of external curves and in some cases slatted wooden seats.

Above. Willowbrook-bodied Daimler COG5 number 35 (DTE 919) is shown alongside Kingsway depot with the Department's first conductresses of World War II. The bus was later renumbered 919. A photograph such as this would have been impossible in later years as traffic increased. *(LCT)*

Below. Awaiting departure from the Bus Station in May 1952 is number 381, a Daimler COG5 with Willowbrook body, new in 1940 when it was numbered 39. *(RM)*

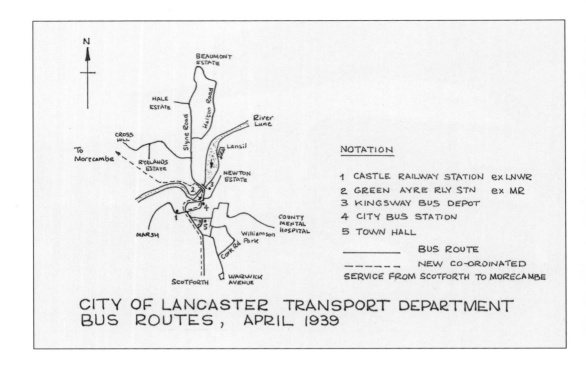

NOTATION

1 CASTLE RAILWAY STATION ex LNWR
2 GREEN AYRE RLY STN ex MR
3 KINGSWAY BUS DEPOT
4 CITY BUS STATION
5 TOWN HALL

———————— BUS ROUTE
— — — — — — NEW CO-ORDINATED
SERVICE FROM SCOTFORTH TO MORECAMBE

CITY OF LANCASTER TRANSPORT DEPARTMENT
BUS ROUTES, APRIL 1939

The allocation of these vehicles was again made by the Ministry of War Transport and operators had no choice with regard to suppliers. The Leyland TD7 was very much non-standard in a fleet made up largely of Daimler chassis. Further north in Whitehaven, Cumberland Motor Services was allocated a number of Guy chassis and three Daimlers in a fleet made up largely of Leylands. Correspondence took place between Lancaster and Cumberland with a view to exchanging the Leyland for one of Cumberland's Daimlers but nothing materialised. No reason for the breakdown of negotiations is recorded but it is suspected that when Lancaster compared the quality and style of the East Lancashire body on their Leyland, which was largely to prewar standards, with the utility Brush bodies on the Daimlers they decided to retain their Leyland. Lancaster may also have been influenced by the fact that the Cumberland vehicles were of the lowbridge type.

Around six buses operated early morning trips on hire to Ribble in the early years of the war to assist in workers transport during construction of a Government 'shadow' factory at Middleton. During wartime Lancaster was allocated a total of nine double-deckers, all being Guy Arab 5LW models with the exception of one Daimler CWG5, and carrying bodies from three different

body builders, Brush, Pickering and Massey Brothers. Of the four 1942/3 Guy Arab I models, three had bodies by Pickering, based in Wishaw, Lanarkshire, a firm normally associated with Scottish operators and whose total output of bodies on Guy Arab I chassis was only eighteen. The Daimler CWG5 and the four 1944 Guy Arab II chassis were bodied by Massey Brothers. Most operators found that the wartime allocations from the Ministry of War Transport were inadequate and they had to resort to hiring vehicles from other operators who, for various reasons, had surplus vehicles. Lancaster's first loan vehicles comprised two Daimler CP6 double-deckers from Wallasey Corporation Motors on hire from June to July 1941 before the arrival of the unfrozen and first utility vehicles. Bolton Corporation had a surplus of vehicles for reasons detailed in the author's book on Bolton Transport and because of this was able to hire vehicles to a number of operators. Lancaster received two Leyland TD3 double-deckers from February to June 1942. No further vehicles were hired during wartime. The last petrol-engined buses in the fleet were withdrawn in 1943.

In late 1944 there was some relaxation of the restrictions on fuel supplies and this in turn led to an improvement in services operated.

Above. Allocated under the Ministry of War Transport allocation system in 1942 was East Lancashire-bodied Leyland TD7 41 (FTB 298), the only Leyland double-decker in the fleet for some years to come. Under the system operators had no choice of vehicle make. Ironically the Leyland / East Lancs combination was later to become the preferred standard in the fleet. *(SLP)*

Upper right. Lancaster was unusual in being allocated wartime bodies by Scottish builder Pickering. The first of these was 43 (FTD 69) on Guy Arab I chassis. It is shown, renumbered 317, heading for Scotforth in October 1950. *(RM)*

Lower right. Massey Brothers of Wigan supplied five bodies on wartime chassis, one on a Daimler CWG5 chassis in 1943 and four on Guy Arab II chassis in 1944. One of the latter, 47 (FTE 66), is shown here in wartime grey livery in Lancaster Bus Station. *(SLP)*

Postwar

One of the earliest events of the postwar period was the renumbering of the fleet which took place in November 1946. Under this scheme vehicles received fleet numbers to coincide with the number part of their registration numbers and this led to some large fleet numbers appearing in a relatively small fleet, even as high as 6560. The first new vehicles arriving in 1947 were all Crossley-bodied and comprised two Leyland PS1 single-deckers, eight Crossley DD42/3 double-deckers and two Crossley SD42/3 single-deckers. Four of the double-deckers, numbered 444-7, were delivered with Brockhouse turbo transmission but had these replaced by standard gearboxes between September 1954 and May 1955. A further four Crossley DD42/3 double-deckers with Crossley bodies followed in 1948. By the end of the forties, the utility bodies on the wartime vehicles were in poor condition whilst the rugged chassis were still serviceable. All were given new bodies by Crossley (5) or by Guy (4) on Park Royal frames between 1950 and 1952. The operational fleet size peaked at 46 following this influx of vehicles.

A new joint operation with Ribble had started in July 1947 when a City Centre to Cross Hill service began.

In 1951 a major change in vehicle policy took place with the arrival of three Leyland PD2/10 double-deckers with Leyland bodies. To date, the only new Leyland double-decker purchased had been the TD7 example allocated to the undertaking under wartime restrictions in 1942. It was a change that was to be permanent for after this time, all new double-deckers were of Leyland manufacture. The last new Daimler vehicles purchased were three single-deck CVG5 models with bodies by Northern Counties of Wigan which arrived in 1952, at a time when front-engined single-deckers were becoming rare as the underfloor-engined types gained popularity. Their arrival signalled the end of an association with Daimler going back to 1925. One of these, No. 466, was converted to front entrance in January 1958 for one-person-operation. In June 1970 it was reseated to 35 seats and retained for use on a service taking prisoners from the Castle Prison to work on the prison farm as it was the only vehicle which could access the Castle gateway. Lancaster, however, obviously had a use for such

vehicles because, in addition to these two new examples, two 1949 AEC Regals of similar layout but with Strachans bodies were purchased from Morecambe and Heysham Corporation, arriving in October 1952 and entering service in January 1953.

The wartime Guy Arab chassis was a stranger to most fleets to which it was allocated under the restrictions which applied at that time. However, it gained a reputation for rugged simplicity and some operators purchased new and updated examples in the postwar period. Lancaster was not one of these but four used examples, new to London Transport, one with Weymann and three with Park Royal bodies were purchased from a dealer in 1953. They appear to have been purchased as a short term measure, retaining their utility bodies, and being disposed of in 1956 or 1957.

No further vehicles were purchased until 1957. By this time the operator had become interested in reviving one-person-operation, which had been in use prewar, and the two AEC Regals from Morecambe were converted for this purpose. The Cross Hill service was selected for this and there followed the aforementioned Daimler conversion which was not considered a success. In order to expand into further route conversions four AEC Regal IV underfloor-engined single-deckers with Burlingham bodies were acquired from Rochdale Corporation Transport. The centre doors were removed by Burlingham and they were equipped for one-person-operation before entering service between March and November 1957. They were Lancaster's first 8ft wide buses. In the same year four new Leyland PD2/41 double-deckers were purchased with bodies by East Lancashire Coachbuilders. This established a relationship with this coachbuilder which was to continue to the end of this era and into the next era of the enlarged operation from 1974 onwards. From this time all double- and single-deck bodies for new vehicles were by East Lancashire Coachbuilders with two exceptions. The first of these concerned the six single-deckers purchased in 1972 which had bodies by Seddon Pennine, brought about by the disastrous fire which took place at East Lancashire Coachbuilders works in 1971 and which disrupted production pending rebuilding of the works. The second concerned the three Leyland Nationals purchased in 1974 and withdrawn in early 1978.

The first new 8ft wide buses arrived in 1958 in the form of three Leyland Tiger Cub single-deckers with East Lancashire bodies and these were followed in 1959 by two similar vehicles. The policy of buying single-deckers, initiated by the change to one-person-operation, continued in 1961 but in this case the chassis were Leyland Leopards, a heavier duty chassis than the Tiger Cub, and again East Lancashire Coachbuilders provided the bodies but in this case they were of dual-doorway pattern with centre exit. In connection with the adoption of one-person-operation, a number of turning circles were provided at terminal points to eliminate the need for reversing.

Services in Lancaster were extended over the years to serve new housing estates. One interesting new service was introduced in 1966 jointly with Ribble and Morecambe and Heysham Corporation to serve the new Lancaster University. It operated as a limited stop service from Morecambe Battery to the University via Lancaster City Centre. The Lancaster share in this service was 22½%. The pattern of other routes in Lancaster was for cross city services to be provided.

From service changes in January 1958, many services did not work back from whence they came, which was not an ideal situation, but one which allowed for scheduling efficiency. The opening of the Lancaster bypass section of the M6 motorway to the east of the city in April 1960 took the A6 trunk traffic away from the city but the Morecambe traffic could still cause snarl-ups crossing the River Lune at Skerton Bridge. To relieve this, from November 1972, Skerton Bridge became one-way inbound and outbound traffic was re-routed as part of a gyratory system over the modified railway bridge which had carried the Lancaster, Morecambe and Heysham electric line until its closure in January 1966. In October 1973 all routes in the City Centre were reorganised following the introduction of a comprehensive one-way scheme. Some buses then had to operate a double loop around George Street and Common Garden Street to enable them to reach certain bus stops, and altogether nearly 50,000 extra miles a year had to be operated to accommodate this scheme. However, on the credit side congestion was relieved and lost mileage became something of a rarity.

Lancaster's first post-war double-deckers were Crossley DD42/3 models with Crossley bodies, eight arriving in 1947 followed by a further five in 1948. Number 569 from the earlier batch heads this line-up in Lancaster Bus Station in October 1964. Behind are number 962 from the later batch and number 572. *(RLW)*

A return to double-deckers was made for the purchases in 1963 and 1965, with Leyland supplying PD2/37 chassis, three examples being supplied in each of these years. The 1965 examples were slightly longer than the 1963 models. The bodies, by East Lancashire Coachbuilders differed from previous double-deck bodies supplied to Lancaster in that they were of the front entrance pattern. Leyland brought out its Panther rear-engined single-deck chassis in 1964 to offer an alternative to the successful Bristol RE, with the advantage of lower and easier entrance. Lancaster purchased three of these 36ft long chassis in each of the years 1967 and 1968 with the East Lancashire bodies reverting to single-door pattern, rather than the dual-door pattern purchased in 1961. The Panther was not the most successful of Leyland's models, falling far short of the standards set by the Bristol RE. Lancaster did not, however, experience the 'flexing' problems experienced by some operators of this chassis and attributed this to the design and strength of the East Lancashire Coachbuilders bodies. For purchases in the years 1969, 1970 and 1972 Lancaster reverted to the simpler and more reliable Leyland Leopard chassis despite its higher frame and East Lancashire again received orders for the bodies. The 1972 deliveries, for reasons previously detailed, had bodies by Seddon's Pennine Coachcraft subsidiary. The final three of these marked a change from 36ft length to 33ft length to cover routes where the longer vehicles were unsuitable.

The desire to offer a low entrance was still there and Leyland in conjunction with the National Bus Company had brought out the Leyland National single-deck model of integral construction and produced at a purpose-built factory near Workington in West Cumbria. The failings of this model, particularly the early examples, have been well documented elsewhere especially with regard to the 0.500 series engine developed for the model which had a reputation for high fuel consumption and also the somewhat spartan finish to the interior of the body. Lancaster purchased three examples, one arriving in December 1973 and the others in March 1974, just in time to pass to the enlarged undertaking as documented in chapter 4.

In January and February 1974, to cover a vehicle shortage, vehicles were hired from Morecambe and Heysham Corporation; one AEC Regent No. 68 and two Leyland PD2s No. 88 and 89 were involved in this.

This chapter in the history of the Lancaster Corporation/Lancaster City Transport came to an end due to Local Government reorganisation on 31st March 1974. At this point Lancaster City Transport was in a deficit situation but offered very low fares, a modern and excellently maintained fleet with a central loading interchange point at Damside Street Bus Station.

Above upper. When new in 1944 Guy Arab II number 47 (FTE 66) carried a Massey body to wartime specification It was rebodied by Crossley in March 1951 and is shown with its new body in Lancaster Bus Station. *(STA)*

Above lower. In 1951 a long association with Leyland double-deckers began with the arrival of three PD2/1 models with Leyland bodywork numbered 708-710. No other make of new double-decker was purchased after this time. Shown in the Bus Station in May 1965 is number 709 (NTC 709). *(RM)*

Left. Three Crossley SD42/3 single-deck vehicles arrived in 1947 and were numbered 613-615. Number 614 (HTC 614) was photographed in Lancaster Bus Station in May 1952. It was withdrawn and sold in May 1958 and the following month operated for the People's League for the Defence of Freedom during the London bus strike. *(RM)*

Management

Reference was made in Chapter 1 to the appointment of Mr WA Tester from Plymouth as Manager and Electrical Engineer in 1903. He remained in post until 1910 when he resigned with effect from 30th November 1910. Mr George C Milnes was appointed as Temporary Engineer for a period of six months from 1st December 1910 and this was made substantive as Borough Electrical and Tramways Engineer from 1st June 1911. His title was changed during 1911 to that of General Manager. During the period 1911 to 1920, Mr WT Charlton held the position of Traffic Manager and it would appear that there was a division of responsibilities at this time. In 1920 Mr Milnes was succeeded by Mr JB Patterson. In the early thirties, a report was prepared by Mr J Barnard, General Manager of Bolton Transport, at the request of the Council to investigate :-

1. The general position of the undertaking to assist the Council in their decision whether to retain control or sell to a private company, and:
2. To investigate the administration of the omnibus undertaking and make recommendations thereon.

Mr Barnard advocated continued control by the Council, subject to a thorough reorganisation of officials and staff, and also that the Department should be self supporting. The outcome was the appointment in 1934 of a new General Manager, Mr JHW Penman, considered to have a better grounding in the industry, possibly suggesting a lack of confidence in the ability of Mr Patterson. There was consternation at the Town Hall over this decision. The suggestions of the Omnibus Committee, which seemingly supported Mr Patterson, were overruled, leading to the resignation of the entire committee. Mr Patterson accepted the position offered to him of Assistant General Manager, presumably at a reduced salary and a position which he only held for a few months. Mr Penman, who had previously been General Manager at Perth, departed in 1937 and became General Manager at Darlington Transport, a position which he held until 1950, the year in which he died.

Mr Penman was succeeded by Mr Charles Smith, formerly Chief Assistant at Leigh Corporation Transport, in December 1937 until his resignation in May 1940. At this time, Mr Alfred Kent was the Depot Superintendent at Lancaster, a position which he had held since 1937, when he had been short-listed for the position of General Manager. He was appointed Acting General Manager in May 1940 and General Manager in June 1941, retaining this until March 1956, when he died. His successor in April 1956 was Mr Albert Burrows, previously Commercial Officer at Portsmouth Corporation Transport, his title at Lancaster being General Manager and Engineer.

In February 1961, Mr Burrows resigned to take up the appointment of General Manager at Barrow in Furness Corporation Transport Department. Mr James Thomas Langley was appointed General Manager and Engineer in April 1961, having previously been Traffic Superintendent and then Deputy General Manager at Bury Corporation Transport Department. Mr Langley resigned in March 1966 to take up the position of General Manager with Preston Corporation Transport, a position which he held until his retirement in 1978. Mr Langley was succeeded at Lancaster by Mr W Cyril Horsefield who had commenced with the Department as a Junior Clerk in 1927, being short-listed for the position of General Manager in 1937, and being appointed Deputy General Manager in 1939, a position which he held until April 1966 when he was appointed Acting General Manager pending his appointment as General Manager in July 1966. He retired in September 1969. Mr Horsefield was succeeded by Mr Brian Godbehere, who had moved from Oldham Corporation Transport in 1969 to become Acting Traffic Assistant at Lancaster, prior to his appointment in 1970 as General Manager (Acting), a position which he held until reorganisation in 1974.

In preparation for reorganisation, and the combining of the undertaking with that of Morecambe and Heysham, Mr Thomas WW Knowles was appointed 'Shadow General Manager' in November 1973 and was reported at the time to be the country's youngest General Manager at the age of 31 years. Further information regarding Mr Knowles is given in Chapter 4.

Upper. Number 466 (NTF 466) was one of three Daimler CVG5 models with Northern Counties bodies supplied in 1952 when new front-engined single –deckers were becoming something of a rarity as underfloor-engined vehicles became popular. *(RM)*

Lower. One of four former London Transport Guy Arab IIs purchased in 1953, Park Royal-bodied number 105 (HGC 105) is shown leaving the Bus Station. *(RMC)*

Upper. In 1957 the Department purchased four AEC Regal IV underfloor-engined single-deckers with bodies by HV Burlingham. These vehicles had been new in 1953. One of them is shown here being inspected on arrival by management and Council members. *(LCT)*

Lower. The first new underfloor-engined single-deckers arrived in 1958 and comprised three Leyland Tiger Cubs with East Lancashire bodies. The first of these, number 175 (175 FTJ) is shown in Lancaster city centre. *(RM)*

Upper. No new double-deckers had been purchased since 1951 and by 1957 Leyland had ceased production of bus bodies. So Lancaster turned to East Lancashire Coachbuilders of Blackburn for the bodies on four Leyland PD2 models, establishing a relationship which was to continue throughout the life of the Department. The first of the four, number 881 (881 BTF), was photographed in the Bus Station in May 1965. *(RM)*

Lower. After two batches of Tiger Cubs in 1958 and 1959 the Department turned to the heavier Leyland Leopard L1, again with East Lancashire bodies, for the 1961 delivery. This comprised three examples of which number 102 (102 UTF) is pictured at the Bus Station. *(STA)*

Opposite page upper. Leyland Panther number 108 (LTC 108F), one of a batch of three with East Lancs bodies supplied in 1968, is shown leaving Lancaster Castle. *(STA/RNH)*

Opposite page lower. East Lancs-bodied Leyland PD2 number 202 (202 YTE) crosses the Chapel Street/ Rosemary Lane junction on North Road heading towards the Bus Station in June 1971. New in 1963 along with 201 and 203, it's arrival signified a change from rear to front entrance double-deckers. *(BD)*

Upper. The 1972 delivery of Leyland Leopards had bodies by Seddon, the order having been diverted following a major fire at the East Lancs works. Number 118 (NTD 118K) from this batch is emerging from North Road in April 1973. *(BD)*

Lower. Three Leyland Nationals were purchased in 1973 and 1974 just before the transfer of the undertaking to Lancaster City Transport. They did not create a good impression and all three were sold to Fishwick of Leyland in 1978. Number 124 (PTC 124M), the last of the batch, was photographed in the Bus Station in March 1974. *(RM)*

MORECAMBE and HEYSHAM CORPORATION
Morecambe Corporation

Despite its title, this chapter commences before the time when the Borough of Morecambe was combined with the Urban District Council of Heysham to form the Borough of Morecambe and Heysham.

Reference to the involvement of Morecambe Corporation in the operation of trams was made in Chapter 1 and we move on from there to consider the operation of buses.

Morecambe Corporation received authority to operate motor buses under The Morecambe Corporation Act 1918 and operation commenced on 1st August 1919 using two Tilling Stevens petrol-electric driven single-deckers. These were followed in 1920/1 by two open-top double-deckers on Leyland RAF type chassis. These buses at first merely supplemented the horse trams until April 1924 when through transport to Heysham was restored with a Bare to Heysham

bus service, operated jointly with Morecambe Tramways Company. Vehicles were garaged at premises in Clark Street. In June 1924 private bus competition started to make itself felt, when County Motors (Lancaster) Ltd. began to operate between Lancaster and Morecambe (West End Road), extending to Heysham in September 1925 when, simultaneously, the Lancaster and District/Fahy's former tram service was also extended there. As a result there were now four bus operators along Heysham Road.

The next buses arrived in 1925 and comprised three Guy BB type chassis with Guy saloon bodies which were used to start the Circular service via Bare village and Lancaster Road, taking in Torrisholme village from the following year. A notable demonstration in September 1925 was of a Clayton Electric bus with 34-seat full-front rear-entrance body finished in Morecambe livery. In 1926 agreement was reached for the purchase of Heysham and District Motors Ltd which had been formed in December 1924 to carry on the Morecambe Tramways Company business after withdrawal of the petrol trams. However, the agreement had to be shelved as Morecambe Corporation did not then have the

An early view of Morecambe Central Promenade and Clock Tower with a single-deck Guy saloon vehicle in the foreground. *(STA)*

CENTRAL PROMENADE, MORECAMBE.

Upper right. Morecambe's first motor buses arrived in 1919 and comprised two Tilling Stevens TS3 models with 30-seat bodies by Brush. Number 1 (B 5981) is shown when new. *(LCT)*

Lower right. Leyland G number L1 (TB 2557) with 43-seat open top body is pictured with its crew when new in 1920. *(LCT)*

Below. Guy BB number G12 (TD 9800) with Short Bros toast rack body dating from 1927 is shown in service on the Promenade near Central Pier in the summer of 1929. It was one of six purchased for tramway replacement. *(RMC)*

statutory powers to operate outside the Borough. In the late summer of 1926 the new 'Ring Road' was opened and named Westgate, along which a new service began. To replace the horse drawn tramway, in October 1926, six Guy FBX 6-wheeler open-top double-deckers with Short Brothers bodies were purchased. These were among the first pneumatic-tyred double-deckers to be built. Two additional Guy BB type single-deckers were also purchased that year and a further two, but carrying 'toastrack' bodies, followed in 1927. These were rebuilt as normal saloons after only one season.

In December 1927 Lancashire and Westmorland Motor Services was acquired by Ribble Motor Services who thus inherited the former Lancaster and District Tramways route between Lancaster and Morecambe.

Heysham and District TC 8766, a Karrier JH, is pictured below on Morecambe Promenade, having been acquired from the Morecambe Tramways Company. *(LCT)*

In the bottom picture a Guy FBX open top double-decker poses for an official photograph when new, not yet numbered and still carrying trade plates. (RMC)

A New Borough

The year 1928 saw the arrival of a further two Guy FBX open-top double-deckers together with one Maudslay and three Dennis single-deckers, two of the latter being 20-seaters for one-person-operation and nicknamed 'Whippets' bodied by JA Cross, a local coachbuilder, and the others by Hall, Lewis. These were the last vehicles to be ordered by Morecambe Corporation prior to the amalgamation with Heysham Urban District Council with effect from October 1928 to form the Borough of Morecambe and Heysham. The shelved agreement to purchase the business of Heysham and District Motors Ltd was now able to go ahead. An interesting application by Heysham and District, rejected by Lancaster Watch Committee in March 1929, was for a service between Heysham and Lancaster. This appears to have been a back-door move towards a municipal service between the towns, as Heysham and District were acquired in May 1929 and included seven vehicles as detailed in the Fleet Summary. The acquisition brought with it a service to Middleton and Overton, outside the new Borough, which had originally been worked by Tourist Motors Ltd and who, it will be recalled, had operated the first motor buses in Heysham. Meanwhile, in February 1929, County Motors (Lancaster) became a subsidiary of Ribble, thus strengthening the latter's position in the district.

The first vehicles ordered by the new undertaking arrived in 1929 and were two further Maudslays with Hall, Lewis bodies and four more Dennis G type 20-seater 'Whippetts' which replaced former Heysham and District Overlands. The original Clark Street garage was now vacated in favour of that acquired with Heysham and District, behind what had been the petrol tram shed on Heysham Road. Permission was given for Maudslay to exhibit a saloon with body by Northern Counties of Wigan, in Morecambe and Heysham livery, at the 1929 Commercial Motor Show, but this was not purchased until 1930.

In 1930 the Corporation opened a new Bus Station at Poulton Hall, by the Market, but it only had limited use by the Corporation's own buses. The Ribble/County Motors terminus of their Lancaster services was transferred here from Queen Square, a short distance away. However, these later transferred to Ribble's new Euston Road Bus Station in 1936, leaving the Poulton Hall site to become a coach parking area.

From October 1931, five years after the trams had finished, the Tramways Department was renamed Transport Department, although the timetable printers were not informed until some years later!

A Maudslay single-decker makes its was along a deserted Morecambe Promenade. *(RMC)*

MORECAMBE
— AND —
HEYSHAM
TRAMWAYS DEPT.

THE
OFFICIAL
TIMES
TABLE.

SEPTEMBER 1st, 1936, until further notice.

Nobody told the printer. The front of the September 1936 timetable shows 'Tramways Dept.' five years after it had been renamed 'Transport Department.'

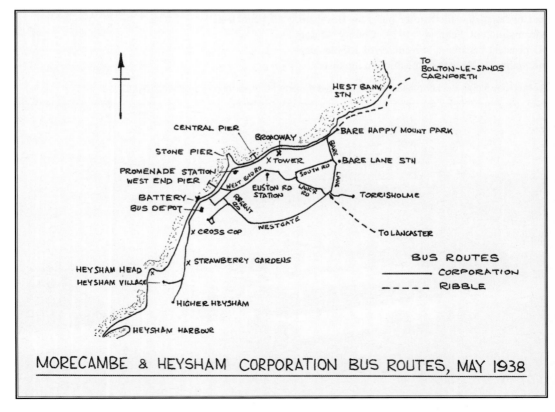

MORECAMBE & HEYSHAM CORPORATION BUS ROUTES, MAY 1938

Mass Demonstrations – a Report by Richard Allen

The phrase 'Mass Demonstrations' normally has political overtones but in this case it concerned double-deck buses. By 1931 the resort had become one of the most popular holiday destinations for residents in the northern parts of the United Kingdom as improved road transport supplemented rail links. The Transport Department was ill-equipped to deal with this influx, consisting as it did then mainly of saloons and obsolete open-top double-deckers, one of which had solid tyres, summarised as below:-

5 Guy BB 30-seaters new in 1925/6
2 Guy BB 32-seaters new in 1927 (rebuilt from toastracks).
4 Maudslay 32-seaters new in 1928/9.
1 Dennis E 32-seater new in 1928.
6 Dennis G one-man 20-seaters new in 1928/9.
6 Guy FBX 53-seat double-deck new in 1926 with 4 cylinder engines.
2 Guy FBX 59-seat double-deck new in 1928, refitted with 6 cylinder engines.
1 AEC 504 (NS Type) double-deck new in 1925.
1 Karrier KL 55-seat double-deck new in 1926, still with solid tyres.
1 Karrier JH 29-seater new in 1924.

The last three had come with the Heysham and District business in May 1929.

The local press was consistently pressurising the Council to improve the fleet, but change was slow. Only five years earlier the horse tramway had been replaced by the six Guy FBX, then among the earliest double-deckers in the UK to be fitted with pneumatic tyres. Such was the pace of development, however, that they quickly appeared obsolete especially when seen alongside Ribble's Leyland Titans.

In the autumn of 1931 the manager, H B Sharpe, was asked to obtain quotations for the provision of top covers or sunshine roofs for the two 1928 Guy double-deckers. The outcome was a suggestion that one of them might be rebodied using a 1927 Roe 69-seat body from a similar chassis just withdrawn by Leeds. No further action was taken on this,

Mr Sharpe was in favour of renewals and with this in mind went to the Commercial Motor Show at Olympia in October 1931 and whilst there, made arrangements with manufacturers for a two week 'in service' demonstration of as many varied double-deckers as possible. On return to Morecambe he reported that the following, presumably Show exhibits, could be demonstrated.

AEC Regent	Roe double-staircase, centre-entrance, of Burnley Corporation
Bristol G	Bristol
Daimler CH6	Brush 52 seats
Dennis Lance	Duple 54 seats, straight staircase
Guy Invincible	Guy 50 seats
Leyland Titan	Leyland 52 seats, highbridge
Maudslay Majestic	Brush 52 seats – Coventry Corporation
Morris Imperial	Brush 50 seats
Thornycroft Daring	Brush 52 seats

The Transport Committee approved this in principle with certain changes to the above. The Morris and Thornycroft vehicles were excluded but a Crossley Condor with diesel engine was added. All the others were petrol engined. The demonstrations were planned to be simultaneous from Tuesday 1st December until Monday 14th December inclusive. Seven arrived in time for a Committee inspection at the depot on 30th November and entered service on 1st December. The Bristol did not arrive in time and entered service on 7th December. Most of the vehicles which entered service were not the ones which had been expected but were as follows:-

The AEC was 26ft long and had a Brush H31/25R body – probably MV 842, later with Westcliffe.

The Bristol was HY 3628 with Roe H24/24R body later with Doncaster.

The Crossley was RG 1676 with Crossley H24/26R camel-roofed body later with Northampton. This did not operate after 12th December.

The Daimler was VK 3418 with Hoyal H26/26R body later with Middlesbrough.

The Dennis was PJ 1576 with Park Royal H26/24R body incorporating a sunshine roof with a roll-back canvas centre section, later with West Bromwich.

The Guy had a Guy H27/24R body but is unidentified.

The Leyland was fitted with a 4.25 inch bore engine, probably an early TD2, and had a Leyland L24/24R body. From 11th to 14th December it was substituted by an earlier TD1 with a 4 inch bore engine and a Leyland H27/24R body, both unidentified.

The Maudslay was a Mentor KV 54 with Ransomes H28/24R body, later to Union Jack then Eastern National.

The demonstrators worked across all main line bus duties in order to equalise mileages and fuel consumption for statistical purposes. As the main line winter timetables only required eight vehicles, these demonstrators, when all were operating, fulfilled that requirement but the Corporation's own vehicles still appeared on other services. All gave good service, the defects encountered were only minor and were not considered detrimental to their general efficiency.

The local press became actively interested and the *Morecambe Visitor* launched a competition to determine which bus the public liked best. In the issue of 9th December there appeared a photograph of the Crossley, confirming it as one of a pair demonstrated when new to Aberdeen. In the issue of 16th December appeared a large

advertisement placed by AEC for the Regent 56-seater and, of course, promoting themselves as builders of London's buses, along with a short article. The Regent was alone among the demonstrators in being to the newly authorised length of 26ft for a two-axle double-deck which, with maximum gross weight of 10 tons, could allow up to 56 seats on an enclosed bus.

Cost considerations were paramount before the Committee made a decision. Mr Sharpe reported that the diesel-engined Crossley was by far the most economical but had the highest purchase price. The most economical among the petrol-engined vehicles was the Dennis. Considerations of chassis and body weight were a major factor, as maximum capacity was sought.

Tenders for the supply of seven buses in various combinations of single- and double-deck were invited. Tenders received totalled nine for double- and eight for single-deck chassis, fourteen for double- and fourteen for single-deck bodies. The press was pushing for more double-decks and the competition result favoured AEC as did Mr Sharpe, their low quotation being the deciding factor. The result was that six AEC Regent double-decks and one AEC Regal single-deck, with Weymann bodies, were ordered although this coachbuilder had not been represented in the demonstration.

Six AEC Regents with Weymann bodies were purchased in 1932 and started an association with AEC that was to last until 1957. They also introduced the new apple green livery. All six are seen at Heysham Village with councillors and officials shortly after delivery. *(BL)*

In January 1932, the Committee decided that nothing less than a new livery would do for the new image and apple green and ivory was chosen. The existing fleet would lose the old red and white livery on repaint. As delivery approached it was arranged to give maximum publicity for the resort and, suitably adorned, the six Regents TF 7465-70 left Addlestone heading north in procession, reaching Morecambe on 22nd March 1932.

They were subject the following day to a handover ceremony outside the Tower, followed by a run to Heysham and return. All entered revenue earning service the same evening. There was nothing but praise for them in the local press which reported that visitors were also highly impressed. Henceforth receipts multiplied. The Regal TF 7464 arrived without fanfare on 5th May 1932, its 32-seat rear platform body perhaps more akin to the existing saloon fleet.

Only two vehicles were replaced by the new arrivals, a Guy 30-seater and the ex-Heysham and District Karrier 29-seater. The total seating capacity of the fleet was thus enhanced by 36% at a stroke. So passed one of the most interesting periods of bus operation in the history of Morecambe and Heysham. The Regents set the standard for years to come, a total of 38 being in operation by the late 1930s.

There was a further demonstration, although not in service, in November 1932 to Morecambe and Heysham and also to Lancaster of the double-deck AEC 'Q' type demonstrator AHX 63 and the operation of a diesel-engined AEC Regent demonstrator from December 1932 until January 1933. An experimental Dorman Ricardo diesel engine was fitted to Guy double-decker No. 11 from 1933 to 1935, after which it was 1945 before diesel-engined vehicles re-appeared. However, petrol-engined double-deckers could still be sampled in service as late as 1959.

The second batch of Weymann-bodied AEC Regents arrived in 1933 and was numbered 35 to 37. The first of these, number 35 (TJ 2490) is shown in the upper picture when new. *(STA)*

Also photographed when new and clearly showing the name of the body builder, this time Park Royal Vehicles, number 45 (CTF 861) was the first of eleven similar buses delivered in 1938. The last vehicles to arrive before the outbreak of war, they carried the Morecambe and Heysham version of the 'modern' swooping style of livery so common in the late thirties. *(STA)*

The Thirties

The accounts for the year ending 31st March 1932 show a healthy situation with a net profit of £6,189, a total of 5,864,203 passengers carried and a fleet of 34 vehicles. The number of passengers carried was the highest to date and the average fare per passenger was 1.67d.

The new Coastal Road, through Hest Bank, was opened and this led to a new service, joint with Ribble, being introduced on 27th May 1933 between Morecambe and Carnforth. When first introduced it was a seasonal service operating until 24th September 1933 and commencing again on 24th June 1934. Because of a fear that this service would abstract business from the main Promenade route and enable Ribble to have a share in the revenue, this service terminated at Lord Street, rather than operating into the centre of the town. The first bus to operate on this service was No. 30 and the crew was driver Emmatt and conductor Brown.

A co-ordination agreement with Ribble in 1934 resulted in, among other things, their Lancaster to Heysham service being allowed to carry local traffic between Euston Road and Heysham, subject to the Corporation retaining that revenue less a mileage allowance.

Between 1933 and 1935 a small number of new vehicles was purchased each year, all AEC Regent double-deckers with Weymann bodies apart from two of the 1935 batch having Park Royal bodies, a make which was to predominate in the next few years. It is also recorded that the four Weymann bodies supplied in 1935 were completed by Park Royal. Further new AEC Regent double-deckers, all with bodies by Park Royal, arrived each year from 1936 to 1938. Two of the bodies on the 1936 vehicles had slide back 'Sunsaloon' roofs and this feature was repeated on all subsequent prewar

double-deckers. These were, however, permanently panelled over during the war. One of these, No. 45, was exhibited at the 1938 Commercial Motor Show and differed in having a streamline livery for a few years. In spite of fleet modernisation, a solid-tyred Karrier double-decker, which came with the Heysham and District business, remained in seasonal use as late as 1935. Morecambe and Heysham remained faithful to the petrol engine at a time when most operators had standardised on diesel engines and all new vehicles supplied prior to the war had petrol engines.

A new depot was built at Heysham Road in 1936 adjacent the existing shed, to accommodate the expanding fleet and, after a further extension incorporating an office frontage, was officially opened on 19th May 1939 less than four months before the declaration of war against Germany. The Autumn Illuminations were becoming ever more popular, Happy Mount Park at Bare being the location for the main tableaux, and putting considerable pressure on the Department at times resulting local coach operators being called in to assist. The Maudslay/Northern Counties single-decker No. 29 was specially illuminated as a mobile tableaux for the 1936 'lights' after which it reverted to use as a bus. From 1937 a withdrawn Dennis saloon No. 17 was fitted out similarly and performed until the outbreak of war put a premature end to the 1939 display.

In June 1938 the undertaking hosted the 37th Annual Conference of the Municipal Tramways and Transport Association. The conference delegates were welcomed by the Mayor Councillor Charles Howes JP, and the President of the Association, Alderman Arthur H Gledhill JP, chairman of Halifax Transport Committee, responded. The proceedings took place at the Central Pier with the conference headquarters being situated at the Grosvenor Hotel.

The new depot building and offices on Heysham Road photographed on the day of the official opening on 19th May 1939. *(LCT)*

Right. AEC Regent number 47 (DTB 66) photographed while demonstrating the opening 'Sunsaloon' roof to officials and members of the Council. *(LCT)*

Below. A group of dignitaries gather in front of 1934 Weymann bodied AEC Regent number 12 (TJ 5788) on the occasion of the official opening of the new depot. *(LCT)*

Wartime

One of the early effects of war on transport operators was a restriction on the supply of fuel and this in turn led to the adoption of emergency timetables giving reduced levels of service generally with earlier finishing times. These emergency timetables came into effect in September 1939 and were regularly revised to take account of worsening or easing of the fuel situation. The Morecambe and Heysham timetable introduced on 1st February 1940 is reproduced and gives advice to passengers boarding and leaving buses in the blackout.

Buses continued to carry the apple green and ivory livery but the white roof was changed to grey in 1941 and soon afterwards the apple green was replaced by a darker Morecambe green relieved only by the grey roof. This situation was short lived and in 1942 two cream bands were introduced. On wartime repaints, the fleetnames were omitted but a coat of arms in a cream 'target' was included.

An early event of wartime in Morecambe was that the Royal Air Force commandeered the new depot for military use and a smaller shed was then built alongside the depot, on the site of the old horse tram shed, to accommodate the fleet.

CONDITIONS

1. Whilst every effort will be made to conform to this Time Table, the Corporation does not guarantee that the Omnibuses will arrive or depart at the times specified, nor will they be responsible for any loss, inconvenience or injury arising from non-compliance with the Time Table. The Corporation reserves the right to alter or cancel any service without previous notice.

2. All Fares and Charges must be paid to the Conductor, and each passenger must obtain a ticket or tickets from the Conductor, showing the amount of fare paid.

3. TICKETS ARE NOT TRANSFERABLE, and must be produced for inspection on demand by any Conductor, Inspector or authorised employee of the Corporation, otherwise the passenger must pay again. Any passenger who leaves the omnibus without paying the proper fare (whether demanded or not) and accepting the appropriate ticket is liable to penalty.

4. All Tickets are issued subject as above referred and on the further express understanding that the passenger is subject to general compliance with the appropriate conditions of the Byelaws, Rules and Regulations, for the time being in force within the Borough of Morecambe and Heysham, and such Byelaws, Rules and Regulations are to be deemed to have been specifically incorporated in such tickets, whether the same have been read by the passenger or not.

MORECAMBE & HEYSHAM CORPORATION TRANSPORT DEPARTMENT.

OMNIBUS TIMETABLE

Commencing 1st February, 1940, to further notice.

WAR EMERGENCY— RESTRICTED OMNIBUS SERVICES.

H. B. SHARPE,
General Manager.

HINTS TO PASSENGERS during the "BLACK-OUT"

TO BOARD A 'BUS.—Stand at a stopping place, ON THE PAVEMENT—close to the edge—and WAVE a white handkerchief or newspaper; or wrap your torch with a handkerchief. DO NOT endanger yourself and others by standing in the roadway or flashing a torch at the oncoming vehicle.

WHEN ALIGHTING FROM A 'BUS—make certain that the vehicle has stopped before stepping off.

Please tender EXACT FARE or STATE VALUE OF COIN.

The co-operation of all passengers is requested during the difficult hours of darkness and in observing the foregoing, passengers will help themselves and greatly benefit Drivers and Conductors.

SECTIONS	WEEKDAYS.	* To Battery Only	SUNDAYS.
Battery to Heysham Village	6-43 a.m., 6-58, 7-13, 7-28 and every 15 mins. to 10-28 p.m.		8-43 a.m. and as weekd'ys
Battery to Princes Crescent & Circular via Central Pier	6-36 a.m., 6-51, 7- 4, 7-21 and every 15 mins. to 10-36 p.m.		8-51 a.m. ,,
Battery to Bare via E.R. Station & Torrisholme	6-31 a.m., 6-46, 7- 1, 7-16 and every 15 mins. to 10-31 p.m.		9-1 a.m. ,,
Battery to E.R. Station (Ribble)	6-41 a.m., 6-56, 7-11, 7-26 and every 15 mins. to 10-41 p.m.		7-56 a.m., 8-26 ,,
Battery to Higher Heysham (Ribble)	6-49 a.m., 7- 4, 7-19, 7-34 and every 15 mins. to 10-19 p.m.		7-34 a.m., 8-4 ,,
Battery to Warley Avenue	8-50 a.m. and every 2 hours to 8-50 p.m., 9-50 p.m.		10-50 a.m. ,,
Bare (Princes Crescent) to Heysham Village via C. Pier...	6-58 a.m., 7-13, 7-28, 7-43 and every 15 mins. to 10-13 p.m. *10-28, *43, *58		9-28 a.m. ,,
Bare (Princes Crescent) to Torrisholme, E.R. Stn. & Battery	6-50 a.m., 7- 5, 7-20, 7-35 and every 15 mins. to 10-50 p.m.		9- 5 a.m. ,,
Bare Institute to Heysham Village via C. Pier	6-56 a.m., 7-11, 7-26, 7-41 and every 15 mins. to 10-11 p.m. *10-26, *41, *56		9-26 a.m. ,,
e Institute to Torrisholme, E.R. Station & Battery ...	6-54 a.m., 7- 9, 7-24, 7-39 and every 15 mins. to 10-54 p.m.		9-9 a.m. ,,
Bare Lane Station (South Road) to Balmoral Rd. Junction	8-30 a.m., 9-30 and 30 mins. past each hour to 10-30 p.m.		9-30 a.m. ,,
Balmoral Road Junction to Bare Station (South Road) ...	8-15 a.m., 9-15 and 15 mins. past each hour to 10-15 p.m.		9-15 a.m. ,,
Central Pier to Heysham Village	7- 5 a.m., 7-20, 7-35, 7-50 and every 15 mins. to 10-20 p.m. *10-35, *50, *11-5		9-35 a.m. ,,
Central Pier to Princes Crescent & Circular	6-43 a.m., 6-58, 7-13, 7-28 and every 15 mins. to 10-43 p.m.		8-58 a.m. ,,
Euston Road Station to Bare (South Road)	8-22 a.m., 9-22 and 22 mins. past each hour to 10-22 p.m.		9-22 a.m. ,,
Euston Road Station to Balmoral Road	8-38 a.m., 9-38 and 38 mins. past each hour to 10-38 p.m.		9-38 a.m. ,,
Euston Road Station to Battery	7- 6 a.m., 7-21, 7-36, 7-51 and every 15 mins. to 11- 6 p.m.		9-21 a.m. ,,
Euston Road Station to Torrisholme & Circular	6-40 a.m., 6-55, 7-10, 7-25 and every 15 mins. to 10-40 p.m.		9-10 a.m. ,,
Euston Road Station to Higher Heysham (Ribble) ...	6-42 a.m., 6-57, 7-12, 7-27 and every 15 mins. to 10-12 p.m.		7-27 a.m., 7-57 ,,
Heysham Towers to E.R. Station via Battery (Ribble)	6-34 a.m., 6-49, 7- 4, 7-19 and every 15 mins. to 10-34 p.m.		7-49 a.m., 8-19 ,,
Heysham Village to Princes Crescent & Circular	6-56 a.m., 7-11, 7-26, 7-41 and every 15 mins. to 10-26 p.m. *10-41		8-56 a.m. ,,
Higher Heysham to Battery via E.R. Station (Ribble) ...	6-56 a.m., 7-11, 7-26, 7-41 and every 15 mins. to 10-11 p.m. *10-41		7-47 a.m., 8-17 ,,
Torrisholme to Battery & Heysham Vill. via (Princes Cres.)	6-48 a.m., 7- 3, 7-18, 7-33 and every 15 mins. to 10 -3 p.m. *10-18, *33, *48		9-18 a.m. ,,
Torrisholme to Battery via E.R. Station	7- 0 a.m., 7-15, 7-30, 7-45 and every 15 mins. to 11- 0 p.m.		9-15 a.m. ,,
Warley Avenue to Battery	9-0 a.m. and every 2 hours to 9-0 p.m., 10 p.m.		11-0 a.m. ,,
Battery to Overton	8-0 a.m., 10-10 a.m., 12-10 p.m., 1-10 p.m. and 10 mins. past each hour to 6-10 p.m., then 8-10 p.m. and 10-10 p.m.		10-10 a.m., 12-10 p.m., 2-10, 4-10, 6-10, 8-10, 10-10 p.m.
Overton to Battery	8-30 a.m., 10-30, 12-30, 1-30 p.m. and 30 mins. past each hour to 6-30 p.m., then 8-30 p.m. and 10-30 p.m.		10-30 a.m., 12-30 p.m., 2-30, 4-30, 6-30, 8-30, 10-30 p.m.
recambe Tower to Carnforth	8-3 a.m., 9-3, 12-3 p.m., 1-3 p.m. and 3 mins. past each hour to 7-3 p.m., then 10-3 p.m.		1-3 p.m., 5-3, 7-3, 10-13 p.m.
Carnforth to Morecambe Tower	8-35 a.m., 9-35, 12-35, 1-35 p.m. and 35 mins. past each hour to 7-35 p.m., then 10-35 p.m.		1-35 p.m., 5-35, 7-35, 10-35 p.m.

Through service between E.R. Station & Higher Heysham, will be operated by the Ribble Motor Services, on behalf of the Corporation, marked (Ribble)

The wartime situation in Morecambe and Heysham provided something of a contrast with that in neighbouring Lancaster. Morecambe and Heysham relied very heavily on its seasonal trade provided by visitors to the resort in the summer season. As a result of wartime conditions the number of such visitors was drastically reduced and the undertaking was not allocated any new vehicles built to the wartime specification and allocated by the Ministry of War Transport. The immediate effect of the war was the shortage of fuel and this led to a reduction in services which could be operated. Despite the lack of visitors it seems that in the early years of the war there was an increase in the number of passengers carried annually and with the enforced reduction in services, this put the undertaking under some strain.

However, the Department found that it had a surplus of vehicles and from a prewar strength of 50 vehicles, only some 30 AEC Regents were now needed to maintain requirements, enabling it to dispose of outdated stock and to hire vehicles to other operators whose needs were greater. The AEC Regents dating from 1932 and 1933 were used for this purpose and the author recalls some of these appearing in Whitehaven when four of them were on hire to Cumberland Motor Services from May 1942 to May 1943. Between August 1944 and June 1945 six vehicles were hired to Venture Limited, Basingstoke and two vehicles

were hired to Crosville from March 1943 to May 1946. A further vehicle, the AEC Regal from the 1932 delivery, went on hire to the Ministry of Supply from 1940 to June 1941. In addition to hiring of vehicles some were sold at this time for further service. Numbers 7, 14 and 15, the three Guy FBX double-deckers with Short Brothers open-top bodies dating from 1926 and 1928, were sold to Cumberland Motor Services in April 1942 for a total of £350. As far as the author can recall, they were not used in normal service but used on internal works services at the Royal Ordnance Factory at Drigg. They had short lives with Cumberland, being last licensed in January 1943 and sold for scrap in April 1944 to Mulholland of Millom.

During these times the neighbouring undertaking at Lancaster hired vehicles from Wallasey and also from Bolton and it seems surprising that use was not made of surplus vehicles at Morecambe and Heysham. Perhaps it was something to do with political correctness, forties style!

Towards the end of the war the fuel situation eased which meant that previous restrictions could be relaxed slightly and a revised timetable was issued with effect from Thursday 26th October 1944 which allowed for later operation of services.

The annual mileage operated, which in 1939 had been over 1,000,000 dropped to 700,000 by 1945.

Park Royal-bodied AEC Regent number 27 (ATF 995), dating from 1936, displays the darker green livery with two cream bands, an arrangement which was introduced during 1942 and remained until 1947 when the number of cream bands was increased to three. *(RM)*

Postwar

An early development in the postwar period was the fitting of AEC 7.7 litre diesel engines to two of the 1935 AEC Regents Nos. 2 and 4, as replacements for the petrol engines, in the Autumn of 1945. The engine in bus No. 4 was fitted in September 1945 and that in bus No. 2 in October 1945. It is said that the extra vibration from the replacement units quickly shook the buses apart and thus had a short innings, but on withdrawal the engines were transferred to 1937 buses Nos. 26 and 44, until the same thing happened again, whence they finally went into 1938 buses Nos. 25 and 49 from 1956/7. The depot building which had been commandeered by the RAF was handed back to the Corporation in 1946.

Due to the restrictions which had applied regarding the supply of new vehicles during wartime, and also a substantial increase in passenger numbers as peace time dawned, there was great demand for new vehicles placed on suppliers. As a result of this delays were encountered in the supply of vehicles.

It was 1947 when the first new postwar vehicles arrived and the Department remained faithful to AEC for the chassis and Park Royal for the double-deck bodies, a total of six vehicles being purchased. These were the first new vehicles to be supplied with diesel engines and this set the trend for future purchases. A further six AEC Regent III double-deckers with Park Royal bodies arrived in 1948 with another twelve in 1949, quite a large order for a small undertaking. The 1948 and 1949 Regents were 8ft wide but provided with seats designed for 7ft 6ins wide vehicles. The seats were positioned away from the inner panels of the vehicles with metal plates fitted to the seat backs to block the gaps and there was also increased width to the gangway. In 1950 two AEC Regal III single-deckers with Strachans bodies were purchased, for a service to Middleton Tower Holiday Camp but this did not materialise, as the camp decided to provide its own transport. As a result they were sold on to Lancaster City Transport in October 1951. In addition to the single-deckers, seven Park Royal-bodied AEC Regent III double-deckers arrived and fleet modernisation was well under way. One of these, No. 72, was exhibited at the 1950 Commercial Motor Show and carried an updated design of Park Royal body. Fleet strength had recovered to the prewar 50 after the 1948 deliveries which meant that withdrawals could start again after the 1949 deliveries.

The autumn Illuminations recommenced in 1949 after the war and its after effects. A withdrawn 1935 AEC Regent was cut down to single-deck and illuminated to promote them. Still petrol powered, it was used to tour industrial towns from the Midlands northwards to mid-Scotland in the autumn period each year until 1960.

From January 1947 a third cream band was added below the upper deck windows and roofs became green and this remained standard until July 1958 when the area of cream was increased to include the window surrounds and the roof. In 1959 the large shaded fleetname on the waistband was replaced by a smaller fleetname on the lower panels but the shaded numbers continued to be applied until around 1961. Exterior advertising began to appear on buses from late 1960.

The year 1951 saw a change of bodybuilder to Weymann but still on AEC Regent III chassis. By this time 39 new vehicles had entered the fleet in the five years since 1947. As a result of this, the intake of new vehicles slowed considerably with three Park Royal-bodied AEC Regent III double-deckers arriving in 1954, these being the last AEC Regent III models to be supplied to Morecambe and Heysham. The fleet strength peaked at 54 for a few years after these were delivered. By 1957 when the next vehicles arrived the current AEC double-deck chassis was the Regent V model and five were purchased with bodies by Massey Brothers of Wigan, a new make for the undertaking. Park Royal had by this time replaced their well proportioned double-deck design by a very austere looking body often regarded as the ugliest double-deck body on the market. A number of regular Park Royal customers, including in addition to Morecambe and Heysham, Barrow in Furness, Ipswich and Southampton, moved away from Park Royal at this time, diverting custom to other builders such as Massey Brothers and East Lancashire Coachbuilders, although Southampton did initially take delivery of examples of the modified Park Royal design.

The early part of the 1950s was generally a period of growth for passenger transport operators with the number of passengers increasing. In

Upper. One of the first post-war batch of AECs, 1947 Park Royal-bodied Regent II number 8 (GTJ 693) arrives at Heysham Village. In the background is a similar vehicle leaving the terminus. *(STA)*

Centre. There is apparently no shortage of passengers as number 79 (TTB 688), an AEC Regent III with Park Royal 8ft wide body, loads at the Battery for Heysham. It was one of three delivered in 1954 and described as 'lightweight', but which were well proportioned and well finished vehicles, the extra six inches width making them look quite different from number 8 above. *(KS)*

Below. Photographed at Strachans' London works prior to delivery in January 1950 are two AEC Regal III single-deckers numbered 52 and 53 (KTF 581/2). They had short lives with Morecambe and Heysham, passing to Lancaster Corporation in October 1951. *(RMC)*

Morecambe and Heysham the peak was reached in the financial year 1955/6 when almost 13 million passengers were carried, possibly due in part to the excellent summer weather in 1955. Thereafter the number of passengers began to decline and at the end of the 1959 summer season a reduction in the fleet size began to take place. At this time, the last petrol-engined AEC Regents were sold, these being by then the last municipally operated petrol-engined double-deck vehicles on the British mainland.

The undertaking must have been pleased with the bodies by Massey Brothers because after this all new double-deck bodies purchased, came from this supplier. However, no further AEC Regent chassis were purchased, thus bringing to an end a period of 25 years during which all new chassis purchased, with the exception of the two single-deck AEC Regals of 1950, had been AEC Regents, quite an impressive record for a small undertaking. The two double-deckers supplied in each of the years 1960 and 1962 were Leyland PD2 models, the first Leyland double-deckers to be supplied to the Morecambe and Heysham fleet. Morecambe had, of course, purchased Leyland G type chassis in 1920 and 1921. They were also the last double-deck vehicles to be supplied to the undertaking. All Regent III and Regent V batches were upseated from 56 to 59 in the early 1960s. In 1961 a service finally started operating to Middleton Tower Holiday Camp after they ceased providing their own transport.

In 1962 it was decided to re-introduce open-top double-deck buses as a tourist attraction in an attempt to increase passenger numbers. The vehicles chosen for this were the two prewar AEC Regents Nos. 25 and 49, which had been fitted with diesel engines in 1956 and 1957. The success of the open-top service was considerable and after 5 years operation Nos. 25 and 49 were replaced by three postwar AEC Regents Nos.62/4/5 with three more Nos. 60/1/3 following in 1968 and with a further example No. 58 being added in 1970.

In the sixties service developments and economies continued apace and the most significant of these was introduced on 13th October 1966. This was a limited stop joint service with Lancaster City Transport and Ribble between Morecambe Battery, Lancaster and Lancaster University. Morecambe and Heysham, together with Lancaster, each had a 22½% share whilst

Ribble had 55%. It was the first time that local authority buses had operated between Morecambe and Lancaster since 1939 when, from April until the outbreak of war, a joint operating arrangement existed between Ribble and Lancaster City Transport.

After 1962 no further vehicles were required until 1967 and from this year onwards, all new vehicles were single-deck, influenced by the desire, or should we say necessity, to introduce one-person-operation. This brought about a return to AEC as chassis supplier and six rear-engined AEC Swift models were purchased in 1967 with bodies by Pennine Coachcraft, a subsidiary of Seddon Vehicles. These six chassis were within the first nine Swift chassis to be manufactured. They were the first vehicles to be provided with route number blinds and were delivered in a new livery of dark green and very light green. These and subsequent deliveries were fitted for one-person-operation. A similar vehicle was supplied in 1968 followed by a further three AEC Swifts with bodies by Northern Counties in 1970.

This revised livery known as Morecambe green and Heysham green was also applied to double-deckers on repaint. The lower panels and a band below the upper saloon windows were in the darker green and the remainder in the lighter green.

AEC was at this time part of the Leyland Motors empire and by 1972 when the next vehicles were required, Leyland had produced, in conjunction with the National Bus Company, the Leyland National single-decker. In an attempt to promote sales of this integral vehicle, Leyland withdrew from the market the AEC Swift, Leyland Panther and Bristol RE, this latter vehicle generally being regarded as the best of the rear-engined single-deck vehicles. Seddon Vehicles had introduced their RU model in an attempt to provide a rear-engined model with Gardner engine of similar specification to the popular Bristol RE. Smaller operators, outside the fold of the National Bus Company, were often reluctant to purchase the Leyland National which they saw as over sophisticated and with an engine which was gaining a reputation for high fuel consumption and this provided a market for Seddon. Morecambe and Heysham took delivery of four Seddon RU models in 1972 followed by a further two in 1973 all with bodies by Seddon.

Photographed above in Euston Road after receiving the later livery with more cream, is 1951 Weymann-bodied AEC Regent III number 76 (MTE 638). *(STA)*

The five AEC Regents purchased in 1957 saw a change in body supplier to Massey Brothers of Wigan. Number 82 (791 ATD), photographed in the lower picture was numerically the first of the batch. *(RM)*

The long established association with AEC Regent double-deckers going back to 1932 was broken in 1960 when three Leyland PD2/37 models were purchased. Massey was favoured for the body order and number 89 (35 MTD) from the batch is illustrated above in July 1967. These were the first Morecambe and Heysham double-deckers to have forward entrances. *(RM)*

Open top Regent number 49 (DTB 68) was new in 1938 and had its petrol engine replaced by a diesel in October 1957. It was converted to open top in March 1962 and in that form is seen below passing Burton's store on the Promenade. *(KS)*

In 1967 a batch of six AEC Swift single-deckers was purchased with two-door bodies by Pennine of Oldham designed for one-person-operation. On a hot summer day, passengers board number 6 (CTJ 106E) (above) outside Euston Road Bus Station on service 6 for Peel Avenue. *(KS)*

There was another change of chassis supplier in 1972 when four Seddon RU models arrived with bodies by Seddon's own coach building arm previously known as Pennine Coachcraft. They were numbered 11 to 14 and number 12 (MTE 612K) was only three months old when photographed (below) in Euston Road on its way to Peel Avenue on service 7 in August 1972. *(BD)*

Two of the 1972 vehicles and the 1973 vehicles were provided with coach seating whilst the 1973 vehicles were in a unique livery of Chelsea Blue and very pale green and were the last vehicles to be purchased by Morecambe and Heysham Corporation. They were classified as dual-purpose and were purchased as a result of the desire of the Corporation to enter the private hire market. However, the Seddon RU was not a successful model and the problems experienced with it by Crosville Motor Services, who had one hundred examples imposed on them by the National Bus Company, have been well documented, although one operator did describe the Seddon RU as being no worse than the Leyland Panther, which itself was not the most successful Leyland model. The Morecambe and Heysham Seddons passed to Lancaster City Council in 1974 but had short lives, being withdrawn in 1977.

The acquisition of these longer vehicles resulted in additional space being required within the depot building. In order to meet this requirement the Department regained partial use of the small building which had been erected at the outbreak of the war. When the threat of nationalisation of the bus industry arose, just after the war, this building had been passed to the Watch Committee for public car parking purposes so that if the Transport Undertaking had been nationalised, the Corporation would have retained this particular asset.

Following withdrawal, 1948 AEC Regent No. 20 passed to the town's Publicity Department, re-emerging in a turquoise and primrose colour scheme in 1973 to promote the resort throughout the country.

The Morecambe and Heysham undertaking had been profitable over the years and the Council did not want to pass reserves to the new Authority and decided not to implement a fares increase in 1973, but to use reserves.

Management

In March 1926 Mr A Eaton was appointed General Manager of Morecambe Corporation Transport, having previously been with Chesterfield Corporation Transport. His reign at Morecambe was short, ending in June 1926 when he resigned. His successor was Mr HCW Ludgate who had been General Manager at West Bridgford Urban District

Morecambe and Heysham General Manager Peter Ellis talks with Ronnie Armstrong, former Deputy General Manager, Albert Burrows, the former General Manager of Lancaster and Vin Rigby, the former General Manager of Morecambe. *(LCT)*

Council Transport. In March 1930, he resigned in order to take up the position of General Manager at Swindon Corporation Transport, a position which he held for 27 years until his retirement. During his time at Morecambe the title of the undertaking had changed from Morecambe to Morecambe and Heysham, following amalgamation of the two Authorities in 1928. Mr Ludgate was succeeded by Mr HB Sharpe, previously Rolling Stock Superintendent and then Deputy General Manager at Rotherham Corporation. He was appointed in May 1930 and remained in office until he died in June 1946.

In July 1946 Mr WHT Marshall was appointed General Manager, having been employed by the undertaking since 1940, first as Traffic Superintendent and then from 1944 as Deputy General Manager. He resigned in April 1957 to take up the position of General Manager at Burton on Trent Corporation Transport and remained in that position until his retirement in 1969. The next General Manager, in office from May 1957 to May 1966, was Mr Albert Vincent Rigby who had been Traffic Superintendent at Wigan Corporation Transport since November 1948. He left Morecambe in June 1966 to become General Manager at Chesterfield Corporation Transport, remaining there until his retirement in 1974. Mr Rigby was succeeded in August 1966 by Mr Peter Alan Ellis, formerly Deputy General Manager at West Bromwich Corporation Transport and he remained in office until June 1972 when he was appointed General Manager at Darlington Corporation Transport, a position from which he retired in 1982. By the time Mr Ellis departed in 1972, reorganisation was looming and Mr George W Stevens was appointed General Manager (Acting) a position which he held until reorganisation in 1974. He had previously been employed with the undertaking as Administration Officer and Deputy General Manager since 1971. Mr Stevens became Deputy General Manager of the new undertaking and remained in that position until his retirement in 1983.

On the departure of Peter Ellis in June 1972 George Stevens was appointed General Manager (Acting) pending the reorganisation of 1974. *(LCT)*

Morecambe and Heysham Corporation

TRANSPORT DEPARTMENT

TIME TABLE

ISSUED

28TH SEPTEMBER, 1959

UNTIL FURTHER NOTICE

Transport Offices,
Heysham Road,
Tel.: Mcbe. 4198 or 4199.

A. V. RIGBY,
General Manager.

LANCASTER CITY COUNCIL

The new era began on 1st April 1974 and brought together the transport undertaking of Lancaster with that of Morecambe and Heysham. As previously reported, Mr Thomas WW Knowles had been appointed General Manager Designate in November 1973 and he was faced with the responsibility of integrating the two undertakings into one.

Mr Knowles had commenced his career as a Management Trainee with Potteries Motor Traction Co. Ltd Stoke on Trent in October 1960 and continued his training with Trent Motor Traction Co. Ltd Derby from May 1963 until October 1966. He then became Traffic Assistant (Research and Development) with Derby Corporation Omnibus Department before moving to Reading Corporation Transport as Traffic Superintendent in March 1971. He was to remain the only General Manager of the new undertaking.

On 26th October 1986 he became Managing Director of Lancaster City Transport Limited and was retained until 5th November 1993 after the demise of the company in order to assist with its winding up, thus completing 20 years to the day from his appointment.

In 2010 Mr Knowles is still involved in the bus business with his Transport Consultancy, in particular being a non-executive director with Newport Transport Limited, and having a regular involvement with Tom Tappin Limited who also operate the Oxford Guide Friday/City Sightseeing Tours with open-top buses. He is, in addition, the part-time administrator for ALBUM, the Association of Local Bus Company Managers.

The two undertakings contrasted sharply in their characteristics. Morecambe and Heysham as a holiday resort relied heavily on tourist trade in the summer season whereas Lancaster's business was fairly regular throughout the year. Morecambe and Heysham was a profitable operation but came with a fleet which was very much outdated, including 27 AEC Regent double-deckers between

A blue and white bus heading along Morecambe Promenade towards Heysham with the name 'Lancaster City Council' on the side epitomises the reorganisation which had taken place. The Alexander-bodied Leyland Leopard was the predominant single-deck model in the fleet and number 304 (MFR 304P) is pictured below on 8th May 1985. (HP)

Thomas WW Knowles was appointed General Manager Designate of the new undertaking in November 1973, becoming General Manager in April 1974. He was the only person to hold that office in this undertaking, becoming Managing Director of Lancaster City Transport Ltd on privatisation. *(LCT)*

17 and 25 years old. On the other hand Lancaster had maintained a low fares policy, came with a fleet which had been regularly updated over the years but also came with a sizeable deficit.

The marrying of the two undertakings was not helped by the fact that they had operated independently with the main services between the two centres being provided by Ribble, at that time a subsidiary of the National Bus Company. This was an unusual situation in Lancashire where joint operation between adjacent municipal operators had been the norm for many years and in many places. Two basic issues which had to be settled for the commencement of operations were location of the head office and the livery.

Both operators had their own attractive liveries, that at Lancaster being ruby red and broken white whilst Morecambe and Heysham had been two shades of green, Morecambe green and Heysham green. Previous to this it had been green and cream and in the latter years Morecambe blue and Heysham green had been used on the Seddon RUs. Obviously there had to be a change from these basic colours and not surprisingly, blue was chosen, the actual shade being Trafalgar Blue with white relief. It has been said that some residents of Morecambe took exception to blue buses operating on the Promenade because 'everyone knows that Morecambe buses have always been green.' (In the early days they had been white and red). Closely associated with the livery was the question of fleetname. Immediately on reorganisation the fleet name *City of Lancaster* was applied to the buses of both former fleets and also to a number of buses as they were repainted in the new livery in the summer of 1974. In the early stages a number of experiments were carried out with regard to detailed application of the new livery but eventually liveries became standardised with the fleetname *Lancaster City Council* applied in lower case lettering, later to be joined by a new City coat of arms in gold. The dual-purpose vehicles were finished in a livery incorporating a greater proportion of white and the rear-engined double-deckers were similarly treated when they arrived in the fleet later.

Initially, the Head Office was established at Morecambe but the accommodation was of insufficient size for the entire undertaking with the result that administration was split between Morecambe and the accommodation at the Kingsway depot in Lancaster. The office of the General Manager was located at Lancaster.

Another priority, which had to be addressed in the early stages of the new undertaking, was the replacement of a large proportion of the Morecambe and Heysham fleet and the former Morecambe and Heysham authority contributed finance towards the purchase of six East Lancashire-bodied Leyland PD3s from Burnley and Pendle Transport, three of which arrived in April 1974 followed by another two in May and the sixth in July. In August four Leyland PD2 double-deckers with Longwell Green bodies were hired from Newport Corporation. These were unusual in being the only vehicles operating in North West England with Longwell Green bodies, a make normally associated with South Wales, although Stockport Corporation had purchased ten examples on Leyland PD2 chassis in 1960. A Metro-Scania saloon was also hired from Newport at the same time as the PD2s for evaluation purposes. Evaluated at the same time was a Leyland National standee

Above. Former Morecambe and Heysham number 56 (KTF 585), a Park Royal-bodied AEC Regent dating from 1949, was carrying the 'City of Lancaster' fleetname on its Morecambe livery when photographed in Euston Road on 24th August 1974 in its 24th year-of operation. *(BD)*

Upper left. When photographed on 6th July 1974, former Lancaster East Lancs-bodied Leyland PD2 number 881 (881 BTF) was operating in Morecambe, still in Lancaster livery. *(BD)*

Lower left. East Lancs-bodied Leyland Leopard number 113 (YTE 113H) displays the 'City of Lancaster' interim fleetname on its Lancaster livery when operating in the city on 29th March 1975. *(BD)*

Above. Number 534 (LHG 534), was one of four East Lancs-bodied Leyland PD3/6s purchased from Burnley and Pendle Transport in 1975. It is shown on Morecambe Promenade heading for the Battery still in its Burnley and Pendle livery. *(BD)*

Upper right. Photographed in North Road, Lancaster in the blue livery is number 841 (HB 9841), an East Lancs-bodied Leyland PD3/4 purchased from Merthyr Tydfil Transport. *(BD)*

Lower right. Heading for the Battery with indicator already set for the return journey to Happy Mount Park on 28th August 1975, is number 411 (411 DKM), a Massey-bodied Leyland PD2/30 purchased from Maidstone Transport. The Maidstone vehicles did not receive the blue Lancaster livery. *(BD)*

demonstrator. Later in the year an ex-Merthyr Tydfil, East Lancashire-bodied PD3 and a Seddon RU single-decker which had previously been a demonstrator before being purchased by Green Bus of Rugeley, were purchased. In 1975 four Massey-bodied Leyland PD2s were purchased from Maidstone Corporation Transport at a time when that undertaking was pursuing a policy of one-person-operated lightweight single-deckers. These remained in Maidstone livery, due to their short stay.

The troublesome Leyland Panthers were transferred to Morecambe depot and found to be more reliable in the flat operating area around Morecambe rather than on the hills of Lancaster. The Seddon RUs maintained their reputation for unreliability and one weekend six of the seven examples were unavailable for service, although it has to be mentioned that two of them had been involved in a collision.

Consideration was given to a major fleet replacement programme and the initial intention was to purchase 12 Metro-Scania single-deckers following the operation of the Newport Corporation example. The order was placed and there followed a visit from a representative of Metro Cammell Weymann who endeavoured to persuade the undertaking to change the order for double-deckers on the grounds that their production line was now jigged for double-deckers. When Lancaster declined to change the order they were advised that they would have to meet additional costs involved in re-jigging the production line to produce single-deckers,

and then also meet the cost of again re-jigging the line for the production of double-deckers. Lancaster was obviously not prepared to do this and cancelled the order.

The order for Metro-Scanias was replaced by an order for twelve Alexander-bodied Leyland Leopards, of varying specification, a type of vehicle which was to figure prominently in the Lancaster fleet in the future with a further 14 examples following in 1977. Although their stepped entrances were a disadvantage on local services, they were more economical and reliable than most alternative designs then available, and they could also undertake Private Hire work, most having tachographs fitted. On entry into service of the first of these in February 1976, the last unconverted former Morecambe and Heysham AEC Regents finally bowed out, a few having been in all-day year-round service to the end. The AEC open-top conversions survived longer. An annual event for these was the Epsom Derby when up to six could be hired out for London area organisers. A few Leyland PD2 open-top replacement conversions were placed in service in 1976/7. In 1977 the practice of giving names to most of the open-top fleet started and was continued with occasional changes. The last open-top AEC was eventually withdrawn after the 1979 season when it was just 30 years old. Also in 1977, the former Lancaster Daimler 466 was repainted in modified fleet livery to work a 'Silver Jubilee' service on Morecambe Promenade. After this, it ceased to be used as a bus but was restored to original livery and retained for special events.

Following reorganisation the Leyland Panthers were transferred to Morecambe, being more suited to the flat territory along the coast rather than the hills around Lancaster. Number 106 (GTC 106F) had received the blue livery when photographed in Morecambe on 7th August 1976. *(BD)*

Above. Alexander-bodied Leyland Leopard number 3045 (MFR 305P) is shown in Damside Street, Lancaster when operating to Hala. *(BD)*

Centre. East Lancs-bodied Leyland PD2 number 201 (201 YTE) heads along Morecambe Promenade towards Heysham after its conversion to open top. At this point it retained its side windows. *(HP)*

Lower right. Preserved Northern Counties-bodied Daimler CVG5 number 466 (NTF 466) in the latest blue livery was operating on the special Silver Jubilee service from Happy Mount Park to Heysham Village when photographed on the last day of operation, 3rd September 1977. *(BD)*

Above. One of the MCW-bodied Leyland Atlanteans with Manchester designed fronts, new to Salford City Transport in 1965, is seen leaving Heysham Village for Happy Mount Park. *(BD)*

Below. Heading along Morecambe Promenade on service 433 to Overton on 8th May 1985 is East Lancs-bodied Leyland Atlantean number 205, a type which typified new double-deckers supplied to Lancaster City Council throughout its period of operation. *(HP)*

Agency Agreement

In the mid-seventies both Ribble, which operated rural and inter-urban services, and Lancaster, were suffering heavy losses and both operators announced major cuts in services. In Lancaster a working party was set up, including trade union representatives, to work out a modified service pattern for the undertaking incorporating major economies. As a result a revised service pattern was introduced in June 1976 which allowed for a reduction in mileage and staff of over 25% albeit with a reduction in passengers carried of 13%. Adjustments took place to this in the following weeks. By 1977 the double-deck fleet had been reduced to ten plus the open-toppers.

Lancashire County Council then stepped in with funding to avoid Ribble's proposed cuts and Lancaster City Council managed to persuade the County Council to support municipal operation as well. Strings were attached to the Agreement which resulted in Lancashire County Council, Lancaster City Council and Ribble setting up a three party agency agreement. Arising from this, the whole network was integrated with no picking up/setting down restrictions enabling all passengers to use the first bus which came, regardless of operator. This did, of course, give Ribble a share of local traffic but it also gave Lancaster, at long last, a share of the trunk Lancaster to Morecambe service. As a result of this, the ten double-deckers were inadequate and both new and used Leyland Atlanteans were purchased. The used examples were ex-Salford vehicles from Greater Manchester PTE and an ex-Trent Motor Traction lowbridge example. These were the first rear-engined double-deckers in the fleet and they were followed in December 1979 by three new East Lancashire-bodied Atlanteans, a type which was to become standard for future new purchases of double-deckers. Also purchased were five Leyland Leopards, three with Duple service bus bodies and two with Duple coach bodies.

The agency agreement was implemented with effect from 1st April 1979 enabling both operators to make economies whilst services were maintained and new links established. Mileage under the agency agreement was allocated in the proportion of mileage previously operated and worked out approximately 45% to Lancaster and 55% to Ribble. Lancaster lost out in this deal due to the reduction in mileage previously implemented.

Three important new links emerged.

The aforementioned former Ribble route from Heysham to Lancaster was extended over the former Corporation Bowerham services and thence to the University.

The former MHCT Higher Heysham - Promenade – Bare – Torrisholme 'Circular' service was extended from Torrisholme through Lancaster to Marsh, giving much improved inter-town frequencies.

The former joint MHCT and Ribble, Carnforth - Morecambe (Lord Street) service was at long last extended through the centre of Morecambe to Heysham and Overton.

City Council buses now appeared further afield on odd journeys of what were hitherto Ribble services from Lancaster to Warton, Brookhouse, Hest Bank and Cockerham. Conversely, Ribble could be seen on what were traditionally Corporation town service in Lancaster and Morecambe. A later introduction was a market day service from Morecambe via Carnforth to Kirkby Lonsdale, just inside Cumbria, worked by the City Council.

In 1980 the last Leyland PD2 open-toppers were replaced by former Salford Leyland Atlantean conversions. Double-deck one-person-operation had begun on 16th June 1980 and the last half-cab double-decker ran in November 1981. The next aim was to achieve full one-person-operation and this was achieved on 1st March 1982. Further new vehicles arrived and by 1983 an additional 16 East Lancashire-bodied Leyland Atlanteans had arrived, the last two being provided with coach seating and high speed rear axles to make them more suitable for long-distance private hire. A further two East Lancashire-bodied Leyland Atlanteans arrived in 1984, the second of these, No. 223, being provided with coach seating, was also the last Leyland Atlantean for the home market to leave the production line.

Further isolated second-hand purchases occurred, notably in 1978 there had been a vehicle exchange with J Fishwick and Sons of Leyland which brought in a pair of Leyland Leopard coaches which had been new to Wallace Arnold, in exchange for Lancaster's three Leyland Nationals. A notable event of 1983 was the return

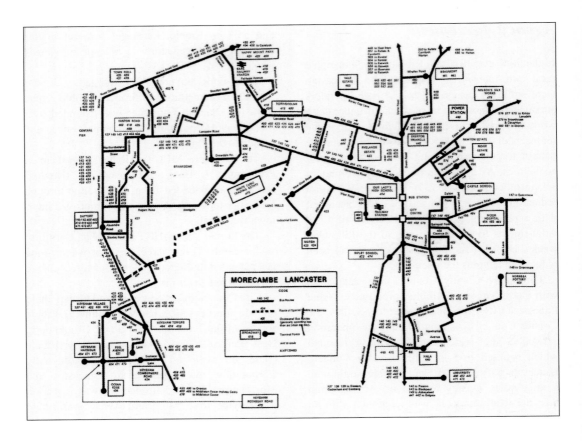

to bus use of former Morecambe and Heysham AEC Regent III No. 20 which, after a few years as the town's publicity vehicle, had been returned and then restored to original livery. It was operated seasonally on a special Morecambe Promenade service.

The fleet had now reduced in size from a peak of 92 to less than 50 with the result that the entire fleet could be housed in the depot at Morecambe. Whilst this entailed some dead mileage, it was cheaper than maintaining two depots. A new office block and workshop were provided at Morecambe and the head office was established there with all other administration facilities in January 1984. The closure of the Lancaster accommodation was a phased process which was completed on 19th February 1984.

The building at Kingsway remained unused for many years, apart from a period when it was used by the Council's Housing Department for the assembly of window frames in connection with the refurbishment of properties. It has since been demolished apart from the frontage which has been retained and incorporated into a new apartment block. It has been suggested that Prince Charles would describe the result as a 'monstrous carbuncle' and some locals refer to it as the 'tangerine' because of its colour.

Following the deregulation of the coaching side of the industry in 1980, a service jointly operated with Lothian Regional Transport, between Edinburgh and Blackpool, commenced in the summer of 1983, operating only in the summer season. Lancaster City Council acted as booking agent and provided a feeder service between Lancaster and Morecambe.

In 1985 Lancaster's vehicles operated to Blackpool and in the following year to St Annes. Another jointly operated service commenced in spring 1985 with Merseyside Transport running between Liverpool and Heysham but lasted only for a few months.

The final new vehicles to arrive in this period came in 1985/6, being Leyland Tiger coaches with bodies by Plaxton (1) and Duple (2). In 1985, four East Lancashire-bodied Leyland Atlanteans arrived from Blackburn Transport, three of these becoming open-toppers to replace some ex-Salford examples.

Above. Seen leaving Heysham Village on service 422 for Happy Mount Park is number 228 (DBA 228C), a Leyland Atlantean with MCW body that had been new to Salford City Transport in 1965. It became fleet number 3074 with SELNEC and then Greater Manchester Buses from whom it was purchased by Lancaster. *(BD)*

Number 222 (BFV 222Y), christened 'Bishop' and carrying adverts for Mitchell's Bitter, was one of two coach-seated Leyland Atlanteans purchased in 1983. In this official photograph it is pictured with the blinds set for the Lancaster University service X70. *(LCT)*

Upper. Five East Lancs-bodied Leyland Atlanteans were purchased from Blackburn Transport in 1985. Three were converted to open top, one being number 85 (UBV 85L) seen on the left. *(LCT)*

Lower. Park Royal-bodied AEC Regent number 20 (JTE 546) is shown here in its preserved state at Heysham Village on 15th June 1991 during a visit to the undertaking by the Cumbria Transport Society. *(HP)*

Deregulation

The Transport Act 1985 was to have a major effect on passenger transport operators throughout the country. On the one hand it included the privatisation of the National Bus Company and on the other hand the deregulation of local bus services, thus removing the protection from direct competition which operators had enjoyed under the 1930 Transport Act. In practice, this meant that operators, both established and new, could register any local service which they considered could be operated commercially (at a profit). Operators were no longer allowed to cross subsidise services and only where the Transport Authority (County Council or Passenger Transport Executive) considered that the level of service did not meet a particular social need, was it allowed discretion to invite tenders for the provision of the service or journeys concerned.

From the same time the restrictive Trade Practices Act 1976 was now to apply to bus services which meant that operation of a joint service by two or more operators, or any joint fares marketing schemes, needed to be registered with the Office of Fair Trading. In the early days, most of these were deemed to be anti-competitive.

Local Authorities were required to divest themselves of their transport undertakings either by selling them to private companies or forming separate 'arms length' limited liability companies. Lancaster City Council decided to retain control and set up a limited company, Lancaster City Transport Limited, with Coopers & Lybrand brought in as consultants to establish business plans etc. The new company commenced operation on 'D Day' 26th October 1986 and at this time the fleet was down to 46 front line vehicles, and a small minibus plus 3 open-toppers and the AEC Regent which was seasonally delicensed. In addition, a new East Lancashire-bodied Leyland Tiger service bus which had been ordered by Lancaster City Council but was delivered to Lancaster City Transport Limited arrived in November 1986. The legislation stated that for fleets of less than 50 vehicles only two executive directors were required and the ruling party on the Council was fearful that if there were more than two executive directors, they may vote with the minority party and defeat the ruling party. The executive directors were Thomas WW Knowles and the financial director, Ian Bevan. The livery was modified slightly by the addition of pale 'Morecambe Blue', often at the expense of white, and a month or so before deregulation Almex 'A' ticket machines had been replaced by Timtronics to give better management information.

Lancashire County Council had been very much against the 1985 Transport Act and published a series of leaflets covering various areas of the County under the general heading 'Your Bus Service is Under Attack'. On the back of the leaflet there was a letter from Councillor Mrs Louise Ellman, Chair of Lancashire County Council, in which she suggested that people of Lancashire may like to write to their Member of Parliament and voice their concerns over the proposed changes. Despite this, the Bill was passed and came into operation on 26th October 1986. Prior to this all operators were required to register with the Traffic Commissioner, by 28th February 1986, details of all services which they intended to operate commercially from Deregulation Day. Details of all these services were listed in a special edition of Notices and Proceedings dated 27th March 1986.

Lancaster developed publicity under the slogan 'Best Bus With Blue Bus' and provided a set of timetable leaflets lettered A to M to cover their services from Deregulation Day 26th October 1986. Details of these services are given in the table below.

Timetable leaflets issued for de-regulation day, 26th October 1986		
Sheet Ref	Route Details	Service Nos
A	Morecambe – Westgate - Lancaster	16, 16A, 16B, 17, 17A
B	Lancaster - Torrisholme - Bare - Promenade - Heysham	23,24
C	Overton - Middleton - Morecambe	28,74
D	Lancaster/Morecambe - Carnforth - Warton – Silverdale/Arnside	59,128,57,58,28,29127,129
E	Lancaster Local Links	
	Marsh Estate	23,24
	Ryelands Estate	43
	Beaumont	50,51
	Vale Estate	53
	Ridge Estate	54,55
	Moor Hospital	54,55
	Hala (Bentham Road)	57
	Hala Square via Newmarket Avenue	70,71,72,73
	Scotforth via Bowerham	X70, X71
F	Halton - Kirkby Lonsdale and Lune Valley	
	Lancaster - Halton	50,51
	Morecambe - Kirkby Lonsdale	127,150,151,152
	Lancaster - Kirkby Lonsdale	574
G	Torrisholme	71,73,23,24,16,69
H	Hest Bank - Bolton le Sands	28,29,57,58
J	University Services	70, 71, X70, X71, 57
L	Bare and Morecambe Promenade	23,24,28,29,69
M	Lancaster - Glasson Dock, Cockerham - Pilling - Garstang	88,89

Operators were not allowed to vary their registrations during the first three months from Deregulation Day. When this three months period expired, Ribble saw its opportunity and commenced minibus operation over some of Lancaster's urban routes commencing in January 1987. Initially, the minibus fleet was primarily 16-seat Sherpas. Ribble at this time was still a subsidiary of the National Bus Company but under the privatisation aspect of the Transport Act 1985, was sold to its management in March 1988.

In retaliation to Ribble's action Lancaster decided to register services in what had traditionally been Ribble territory and on 2nd March 1987 introduced a limited stop 'Fastlink' service from Morecambe to Preston. On 13th April a similar service from Morecambe to Blackpool was introduced. Both became 'all stops' from 30th November and from 31st May 1988 both of these services were extended to start from Middleton Tower or Ocean Edge and a 'Fastlink' service was introduced from Preston to Blackpool via Kirkham. From 16th July Preston Bus introduced a similar service, the timings for which appeared to have been co-ordinated with the LCT timings. In addition a tendered service was obtained from Lancashire County Council for Sunday operation between Preston and Southport, on what was part of Ribble limited stop service 727. It was operated as an extension to the Morecambe to Preston service.

From 24th October a Winmarleigh – Garstang service commenced, supplementing the Garstang – Preston section of the Morecambe service and connecting at Garstang with the Morecambe – Blackpool service.

To boost the fleet for these and tendered services, in 1987 batches of Alexander-bodied Leyland Atlanteans were acquired from Bournemouth and from Fife Scottish, the latter having been new to Aberdeen.

National Express

A National Express contract was won and commenced on 26th April 1987 when service 352 Blackpool – Nottingham was worked on a daily round trip basis. From October 1987, this contract gave way to an alternate-day cycle on service 351 Blackpool – Great Yarmouth, which involved an overnight stay, returning the next day. This continued until the end of April 1988.

The coach employed, usually Leyland Tiger No. 99, worked the first X42, later 42, Morecambe – Blackpool service and the last return journey, which enabled overnight servicing at Morecambe, while a variable LCT vehicle was outstationed at the Rigby Road, depot of Blackpool Transport to work in conjunction with the National Express coach.

The solitary East Lancs-bodied Leyland Tiger in the fleet, number 154 (D154 THG) leaves Lancaster Bus Station for Warton on 8th September 1989. *(RM)*

Upper right. Number 222 'Bishop' again, this time arriving in Blackpool from Morecambe on service X42, prior to working National Express service 351 to Great Yarmouth on 31st August 1987. *(RM)*

Lower right. Former Bournemouth Corporation Alexander-bodied Leyland Atlantean number 246 (SEL 246H) leaves Lancaster Bus Station for Heysham Towers on 8th April 1989. *(RM)*

Below. Duple-bodied Leyland Tiger number 99 (B99 YRN) prepares to leave the depot to operate service X42 to Blackpool from where it would work National Express service 352. *(LCT)*

Lancaster in Cumbria

Lancaster then entered into discussions with Barrow Borough Transport Limited, which had also suffered from the entry of Ribble into its traditional territory, with a view to operating town services in Kendal. Operations commenced on 30th November 1987 under the combined 'Blue Bus' network competing with Ribble on both town and inter urban services to Lancaster and South West Cumbria. The initial services operated Mondays to Saturdays and the network provided is show below.

Lakeland services at 30th November 1987

4	Barrow-Ulverston-Grange over Sands-Kendal (3 journeys/day – B)
5	Lancaster-Canforth-Warton-Holme-Milnthorpe-Kendal (7 journeys/day – L)
6	Morecambe-Carnforth-Warton-Milnthorpe-Oxenholme-Kendal (1 journey/day – L)
7	Lancaster-Canforth-Warton-Milnthorpe-Kendal (1 or 2 journeys/day – L)
8	Kendal-Windermere Road-Hall Garth-Burnside Road-Kendal (Every 15 minutes – BL)
9	Kendal-Railway Station-Sandylands Estate (Every 15 minutes – BL)
B	– Operated by Barrow Transport
L	– Operated by Lancaster Transport

Return fares were introduced at LCT's standard rate of 1½ times the single fare and Ribble responded similarly and also withdrew peak surcharges. Three buses were required at any one time on the town services with each operator providing about half the journeys on services 8 and 9. However, Barrow decided during the first week, that it did not wish to continue with the operation and by Christmas had registered with the traffic commissioner its intention to discontinue its part in the scheme with effect from 6th February 1988. Barrow had designed attractive publicity for the operation and their Leyland Nationals had destinations included on the blinds. Lancaster had been responsible for the timetabling and normally provided Alexander-bodied Leyland Leopards for the service, usually the ones with high back seats. A number of ex Trent Leyland Leopards with Alexander 'T' type bodies

arrived from early 1988 and became the preferred vehicles for these services.

The withdrawal of Barrow meant that from 8th February 1988 Lancaster was on its own in the fight with Ribble in Kendal. Town services 8 and 9 continued to operate on a frequency of 15 minutes but the Hall Garth service operated via Windermere Road in both directions and each route was given a few later departures. In order to continue operation Lancaster had to increase the number of buses provided and the opportunity was taken to strengthen the more promising service 7 via Oxenholme at the expense of service 5. In total, Lancaster now had 14 southbound departures from Kendal on Mondays to Saturdays whilst an extension giving a service for Queen Katherine School on the Appleby road was retained, giving an additional service 7 journey to Milnthorpe on schooldays.

As LCT became established in Kendal, the public made it clear that a demand existed for services north from Kendal into the Lake District. The proposal seemed practical but through working beyond Kendal would put an end to the inter working of the town services with the Lancaster to Kendal workings. As a result of this it was decided to open an outstation in Kendal which had the added advantage of local staff becoming better known to the passengers. The outstation opened on Tuesday 31st May 1988 and this resulted in a new network of services as follows:-

---

Lakeland services at 31st May 1988

4	Levens Village-Kendal (Queen Katherine School). (1 return trip schooldays only)
5	Lancaster-Canforth-Warton-Holme-Milnthorpe-Kendal (2 return journeys Mon-Sat)
6/7	Lancaster-Canforth-Warton-Milnthorpe-Oxenholme-Kendal-Burnside-Windermere-Bowness (6)-Ambleside (7) (Hourly Mon-Sat) (Approximately 4 journeys each way extended to Morecambe)
8	Kendal-Windermere Road-Hall Garth (4 per hour)
9	Kendal Railway Station-Sandylands Estate (4 per hour)
X6	Kendal-Blackpool (Limited stop)
X7	Kendal-Blackpool (Limited stop) (1 return journey Weekdays)

Above. Alexander-bodied Leyland Leopard number 317 (WCW 317R) was one of the vehicles allocated to the Kendal depot and is shown here operating on service 9 to Sandylands. *(RM)*

Centre. Purchased from the Trent Motor Traction Company, number 110 (PRA 110R), is seen in Kendal operating a service 6 journey to Lancaster on 4th June 1988. *(RM)*

Lower right. Leyland Leopard number 17 (MRF 17P) with Alexander dual-purpose body leaves Kendal on 29th June 1989 while operating on the extended service 6 from Ambleside to Lancaster. *(HP)*

Most of the through working was operated from Morecambe depot whilst the Kendal outstation, under the control of a leading driver, operated the local services with the subsequent addition of Bingo buses to Lancaster and some shopping excursions. The outstation comprised a parking area with refurbished office, located on the Mintsfeet Industrial Estate. Fuel was obtained from nearby Cumbria Fuels and to assist driver changeover and fuelling, services 8 and 9 no longer operated at a regular 15 minutes frequency.

Operations commenced from Kendal outstation when bus 315, an Alexander dual-purpose bodied Leyland Leopard, left the depot on the Hall Garth service. The first day's allocation comprised 315, similar vehicle 318 and 19, basically the same but to coach specification. When possible, a fourth vehicle was made available from Morecambe as standby. It had been realised that smaller vehicles would be better suited to the Kendal estates and the Town Hall stand and 4 shortened Bedford YRQ models with Duple bodies were acquired from Cleveland Transit, the first, No. 365, entering service in the first week in June with the others following later. During June 1988 there were 73 buses licensed for service, an increase of about 55% since deregulation.

Prior to embarking on the Kendal operation, blue buses had appeared in Kirkby Lonsdale, Cumbria on commercial work and on tendered operations for Lancashire County Council. A new operation from the start of the school term in September 1988 was a commercial journey linking Kirkby Lonsdale, Queen Elizabeth Grammar School with Ingleton, Bentham and Burton in Lonsdale operated by Kendal outstation. One all-day bus also worked on the Ambleside service and a month later another trunk working was transferred to Kendal outstation at which time the summer services ceased and other changes were implemented.

A further town service numbered 10 was introduced from 3rd October between the Town Centre and Heron Hill and on 14th November a Fridays-only service numbered 3 was introduced between Kirkby Lonsdale and Kendal . There was a single return journey operating via the B6254 road, through Old Hutton, the first time for many years that a bus service had operated along that road. With effect from 28th November

1988 improvements were made to town services 8 and 9 and from the same date, service 4 operating between Kendal and Levens at peak times was withdrawn and some minor modifications were made to services 5, 6 and 7 between Kendal and Lancaster.

There were further revisions to services with effect from 20th February 1989 when a new timetable leaflet titled 'Kendal and the Lakes' was introduced. This contained the following services :-

---

Lakeland services at 20th February 1989

3	Kendal-Kirby Lonsdale. (One return journey Friday only)
5	Lancaster-Carnforth-Burton-Milnthorpe-Kendal (One return journey Mon-Sat)
6	Lancaster-Carnforth-Milnthorpe-Oxenholme-Kendal-Bowness-Ambleside (Hourly Mon-Sat), two journeys each way extended to Morecambe)
7	Lancaster-Carnforth-Milnthorpe-Oxenholme-Kendal-Ambleside (One return journey Mon-Sat)
9	Hall Garth-Kendal town centre-Sandylands (Every 13 to 20 mins Mon-Sat))
10	Queen Katherine School journeys

Lancaster City Transport considered that their presence in Kendal had brought benefits to the travelling public with more buses and lower fares and there had also been the provision of employment for local people. It also considered that it had fulfilled many of the objectives of the Government's deregulation policy.

However, as detailed below a period of co-operation with Ribble was entered into and one of the consequences of this was the cessation of the Kendal and Lake District services and the closure of the Kendal outstation. Operation of the Kendal town services ceased on 29th July 1989 and some changes were made to services 5, 6 and 7 which were subsequently withdrawn on 2nd September 1989, the outstation being closed on the same date.

Despite this, Lancaster still operated into Cumbria with services to Kirkby Lonsdale from Lancaster and Settle.

Lonsdale Coaches, Heysham

On 1st July 1988 there was further expansion with the acquisition of Lonsdale Coaches, Heysham, bringing in a further 26 vehicles. One of the reasons for this was a desire to bring Lonsdale director Alan Hewlett into the fold but unfortunately, shortly afterwards he developed cancer and died. Initially, this operation continued as a separate entity from its base at Middleton Road, Heysham but was transferred to Heysham Road Depot in Morecambe, from 28th February 1990. A new coach livery was introduced at this time, white with red, blue and yellow stripes. During the period 1988-93 several vehicles were transferred from the LCT fleet and others were acquired. Leyland Tigers replaced Leopards and AEC Reliances and a Leyland Royal Tiger Doyen, new to Cambus, also arrived. More former Aberdeen Leyland Atlanteans were purchased but, unlike earlier examples, came via Highland Scottish and received advertising liveries.

This acquisition brought another interurban service into the company with the City Flyer service which operated from East Lancashire to connect with the Isle of Man ferries at Heysham Harbour. In the early 1990s this service was amended to operate seasonally as service 100 from Bacup to Heysham. Later service 200 from Leeds and service 300 from Halifax were added and branded as 'Roses Express'. For a period there was an extension of the Leeds service to Doncaster and this continued to operate after the Stagecoach takeover with the Yorkshire terminus being changed to York before the service was withdrawn. At the end of LCT ownership in August 1993, there were 15 vehicles operating.

Upper. Named after the Beatrix Potter character Tom Kitten, number 364 (HPY 364N), a short Bedford with Duple body, formerly with Cleveland Transit, was seen in Kendal on 29th June 1989 while operating on town service 9 to Hall Garth. *(HP)*

Lower. Plaxton-bodied AEC Reliance coach PRD 34, pictured in Cromer, was one of the vehicles taken over with the Lonsdale Coaches business. *(HP)*

Former Cumberland Motor Services Alexander-bodied Leyland Tiger 644 (WAO 644Y) stands in Doncaster Bus Station on service 200 to Morecambe, a location it would have visited with its previous owner on the National express service from Doncaster to Inverness. *(LCT/MF)*

Co-operation with Ribble

Under the privatisation of the National Bus Company, Ribble Motor Services was sold to its management with effect from March 1988. It became clear to both operators that this level of competition could not continue and, shortly before Ribble's management sold the business to Stagecoach, in April 1989, discussions took place which led to the inter-working of services on Sundays and Bank Holidays, with effect from 24th March 1989. On these days return tickets and Lancaster John O'Gaunt/Ribble Explorer tickets became inter available on the co-ordinated services which were numbered in a special 2** series. The intense competition remained during the rest of the week. The services concerned were those operating between Lancaster, Morecambe/ Heysham including the services from Preston and Blackpool to Morecambe.

Following the takeover of Ribble by Stagecoach, further integration of services took place being complete by October 1989 and as previously mentioned, one of the consequences was the closure by Lancaster of the Kendal outstation. As part of the new network, Lancaster commenced operation of minibuses using Optare City Pacers based on the Volkswagen chassis, eventually operating a fleet of twelve before introducing the larger Optare Metrorider. The inter-availability of tickets was applied to all days

and not just Sundays. A notable LCT acquisition in 1989 was an Alexander-bodied Leopard which returned to the fleet after a six-year absence at Eastbourne and which operated in Eastbourne livery for a while. During these years it was not unusual for second-hand acquisitions to operate in 'as acquired' livery, pending repainting.

Many of the older buses were sold and the age profile of the fleet was reduced by the purchase from Greater Manchester Transport of their only three Ailsa double-deckers with Northern Counties bodies. The coach fleet was also upgraded and a revised bus livery with more white and two shades of blue was introduced. In 1992 there arrived the only new vehicles ordered by the company, three Optare Metroriders with K--- LCT registrations.

Despite the agreement with Ribble, the results for the year 1990/1 were not good but a profit of £76,600 was achieved for the year 1991/2 and a profit of £96,600 for the year 1992/3. In an attempt to attract passengers in 1992, reduced fares were offered for off-peak travel but the increase in passengers was insufficient to compensate for the reduced fares. After a month Lancaster withdrew from the scheme but Ribble wished to continue and, as a consequence of this, Lancaster stopped accepting Ribble return tickets. However, two weeks later, Ribble conceded the point and returned to normal fares.

Upper. Optare 'City Pacer' minibus number M3 (E213 PWY) passes the entrance to the Ribble offices in Cable Street, Lancaster. *(HP)*

Lower. When preserved AEC Regent III number 20 was brought back into service, Alexander dual-purpose bodied Leyland Leopard number 20 (MFV 20R) acquired a 'R' suffix to its fleet number, clearly visible in this view as is the dual-purpose livery. *(HP)*

Upper. This experimental livery was applied to East Lancs-bodied Atlantean number 200 (TCK 200X) as shown as it leaves Lancaster on service 272 to Heysham Towers. *(HP)*

Lower. Illustrating the revised livery introduced in 1989, Atlantean number 206 (LFV 206X) is seen loading in Lancaster while working service 42 from Blackpool to Middleton Pontins. *(HP)*

Privatisation

The Government indicated in April 1992 its intention to encourage local authorities to sell their transport undertakings and in June 1992 the Minister for Public Transport made a statement confirming this intention. Shortly after this the City Council received enquiries from some potential bidders including Stagecoach.

At this time Ribble owned two depots in the Lancaster area, one at Skerton, Lancaster and the other at South Avenue, Morecambe. It was looking for a larger site on which to build a new single depot to serve the whole area and enable it to achieve economies of operation.

In September 1992 the Chairman of Stagecoach wrote to Bill Pearson, the Town Clerk of Lancaster, about the possibility of Stagecoach acquiring an interest in Lancaster City Transport, a similar approach having been made to other local authorities owning bus companies. Subsequent to this there was a meeting between Brian Souter and Barry Hinkley of Stagecoach and the Town Clerk to discuss the situation and a further meeting took place in November, although it seems that this second meeting was more concerned with the discussion regarding the off peak fare concessions mentioned earlier. In the wake of the interest from Stagecoach and other interested parties, the City Council passed a resolution on 16th December 1992 to proceed with the sale of its transport undertaking by open tender. Coopers & Lybrand were appointed to prepare tender documents, administer the bidding procedure and advise on the merits of the various bids. The tender documents were prepared on the basis that the City Council would consider bids for the whole group or separately for Lancaster City Transport and Lonsdale Coaches. Reference was also made to the fact that the decision to sell was in response to the Government's policy.

The intention to sell was formally announced at the end of February 1993 and the documents were circulated to all major national bus operators and to those in North West England, with indicative offers being required by 31st March 1993. Initially, there were 14 expressions of interest and eight offers were received, with final offers being invited from five of these organisations with a return date of 22nd May 1993, later brought forward to 12th May 1993. Although it received tender documents, Stagecoach decided not to make an offer because of the possibility of it being referred to the Monopolies and Mergers Commission. Stagecoach also decided that, rather than seek a site for a new depot, it would be an attractive solution to purchase the Heysham Road Bus Depot which was of a size which would meet its need for larger premises.

Stagecoach was also concerned that another major operator may purchase Lancaster City Transport and provide competition in an area where it was well established. Accordingly, on 7th April 1993, Stagecoach registered services on two routes, then jointly operated with Lancaster City Transport, with a view to commencing operation on 21st June 1993. In a press notice released on 21st April 1993, Stagecoach announced that it would not bid for Lancaster City Transport and also announced the additional services to commence on 21st June 1993, stating that once in place Ribble would consider substantial changes to fares and ticket arrangements. These measures were described in the press notice as 'defensive measures' and the notice also declared that Stagecoach would defend its share vigorously if Lancaster City Transport was acquired by a company merely interested in sparking off bus wars in the area.

At a meeting on 28th April 1993 with the Town Clerk and Coopers & Lybrand, Stagecoach explained why it had decided not to bid for Lancaster City Transport and why it had registered services over certain routes. It was as a result of this meeting that the City Council decided to bring forward the tender return date from 22nd May to 12th May 1993.

The Stagecoach bid submitted on 4th May 1993 covered purchase of the depot, 20 buses, assumption of the lease liabilities on three Optare Metrorider minibuses and the purchase of plant and stock. Some revisions were made to the offer in negotiations with the City Council after 4th May 1993.

The City Council had been advised that the likely sale price for the operation as a going concern was between £850,000 and £1,250,000. In the event, the highest offer received for purchase was from Blackpool Transport Services Limited, the municipally-owned bus operator in Blackpool and this was in the sum of £899,000. MTL Trust Holdings, a substantial bus operator based on

Merseyside had also shown interest. However, in view of the press release by Stagecoach and also the registration of services by them, the City Council allowed the other bidders to reconsider their offers, requesting that the revised figures be submitted by 17th May 1993. Blackpool submitted a revised bid of £809,000 but MTL asked for further time to consider their offer.

At its meeting on 17th May 1993, the Policy Committee considered the offers which had been received and compared these with the total amount likely to be received by liquidating the company and selling assets as previously described to Stagecoach. The City Council decided that if the bidding process was further prolonged Stagecoach may withdraw its offer and in view of this decided to wind up Lancaster City Transport and accept the offer of Stagecoach for assets. This was 'reluctantly agreed' by the Department of Transport, after the City Council pointed out that this would provide an orderly rundown of Lancaster City Transport and avert its possible collapse into bankruptcy.

There was no arrangement for Stagecoach to take on staff from Lancaster City Transport, but Stagecoach indicated that it would welcome applications from such staff. Lancaster City Transport ceased trading on 22nd August 1993 and all employees were made redundant. The final day being a Sunday, fortuitously meant that vehicle requirements were low which enabled 13 of the Alexander-bodied Leopards, to be collected that afternoon by their new owner Clydeside 2000 and make space for Stagecoach to move vehicles from South Avenue.

On the final evening of LCT operation, the ex-Southdown PD3 worked on the Higher Heysham – University service while the Regent III worked the Overton – Carnforth service, both, of course, being crew operated and replacing the scheduled OPO vehicles. The Regent actually reached the Battery and depot a few minutes late, just after midnight and into the next day. LCT vehicles finishing duty on the last day, and others still awaiting disposal, were taken to the now vacated South Avenue depot yard, by arrangement with Stagecoach who needed all the available space at Heysham Road. Ribble advertised for a depot engineer and staff 'to take charge of premises new to the company' and commenced operations from Heysham Road Depot on 23rd August 1993,

having vacated their South Avenue premises on 22nd. Shortly afterwards the site was redeveloped for a new supermarket.

In the end Stagecoach bought only ten Atlanteans and took over two of the three 1992 Metroriders which had recently lost their K--- LCT registrations. The Metroriders were in advertising liveries and continued to operate locally but the Atlanteans were transferred to Preston depot.

In the meantime, Lonsdale Coaches had been sold on 20th August as a separate concern to Shaws Coaches of Silverdale along with 12 vehicles. The new owners retained Lonsdale Coaches as a separate unit operating from a new base at Heysham Industrial Estate until 1995. The fleetname continued to be seen until the owners rebranded the whole fleet as 'The Travellers Choice' in 1997. It may be noted that this was not the first municipal coach operation which Shaws had acquired, Hadwins Tours having been bought from Barrow Corporation in 1977.

The last service from Overton to Carnforth on 22nd August 1993 was operated by preserved AEC Regent III number 20. It is shown here ready to depart from Overton. *(RA)*

Nearly there. The crew of No. 20 pause for breath at Carnforth before returning to depot and then it really is the end as No. 20 is parked by Mr Knowles at the depot just after midnight on 22nd/23rd August 1993. *(both LEP)*

Post Privatisation

This was not, however, the end of the story. On 3rd August 1993 the Secretary of State for Transport had asked the Monopolies and Mergers Commission to investigate and report on a possible merger between Lancaster City Transport and Stagecoach Holdings plc. The enquiry was then commenced at great expense to Lancaster City Council, Stagecoach and the taxpayer and proceeded to examine the whole story leading to the merger, concluding its findings on 2nd November 1993.

As might be expected, in a situation such as this, the conclusion was a long drawn out affair and extended to 15 pages. At the end Stagecoach was required to give certain undertakings with regard to frequency of services, fares and attitude to any competitors who registered services on routes which they were operating. Stagecoach argued that this was not necessary as these matters were covered by the Competition Act 1980. However, it was stated that if these undertakings were not forthcoming, Stagecoach would be required to undertake the divestment of the Heysham Road Depot.

Ribble had in effect succeeded in gaining control of the major part of bus services in the Lancaster City Council area and settled down to operate the services with very limited competition. This remained the situation until 1st February 1997 when Stagecoach transferred the Lancaster and Morecambe area from Ribble to Cumberland Motor Services, with the result that from that time the services in the area were controlled from Whitehaven, rather than Preston, and the fleetname Stagecoach Lancaster was adopted. At this time Ribble had been in trouble with the Traffic Commissioner resulting in a reduction in the number of operating discs from 420 to 400 at a time when they wanted to integrate the former Hyndburn operations with their own. To some extent this was a repeat of the situation which Ribble had found itself in eight years earlier when, having gained control of the Barrow area, the operation was then transferred to Cumberland Motor Services. The operations manager at Lancaster, Michelle Hargreaves sent a letter to staff explaining the change.

The result of all this was that Cumberland Motor Services which, until 1986, had been a very local company operating mainly in West Cumbria, now found itself with an operating area extending from north of Carlisle across to Newcastle upon Tyne and southwards to Blackpool and Southport

as Lancaster provided two out of the five vehicles required for Stagecoach Express service X51 from Morecambe to Southport. An interesting point is that at Southport contact was made with the other CMS – Crosville at that time operating jointly with North Western from Chester to Banks via Liverpool and Southport.

Whilst this concludes the history of municipal bus operation in Lancaster and Morecambe the latest development did provide local identity with the adoption of the Stagecoach Lancaster operating name.

Postscript

Stagecoach vacated the old Ribble depot at Skerton, Lancaster, for sale to developers after operations on 4th December 1999, transferring all operations to Heysham Road. However, on 2nd July 2000, Heysham Road was vacated and operations transferred to a new depot at White Lund Industrial Estate, mid way between Lancaster and Morecambe. There was now one new depot in place of the four which had existed some 16 years earlier, two belonging to Ribble and two to the City Council.

Adjacent to Heysham Road depot, as late as July 2000, traces of the tram tracks were still to be seen where the Morecambe Tramways Company petrol tram shed had stood. The 1939 Damside Street Bus Station in Lancaster was closed after use on 24th April 2000 for demolition of its art deco structure. The island platform had gone several years earlier as part of a plan to house a temporary market on the old Ribble side and use only the through bay side, this being modified into reversing bays. A new Bus Station was built on the same site and opened on 18th March 2001.

In May 2005 one of the standard Alexander-bodied Leyland Olympians was painted in the first postwar Morecambe and Heysham livery with appropriate shaded fleetnames but without the coat-of-arms. It retained this livery until withdrawal in early 2010.

All was not quite gone, however, for one of the former Morecambe and Heysham open-top Regents re-appeared locally in 2009 in a pseudo-London Transport type livery but the owner has plans to return it to Morecambe and Heysham livery.

Several Lancaster and Morecambe & Heysham vehicles also exist in private ownership in various parts of the country although some have sadly disappeared over the years.

Opposite page. Number 200 (TCK 200X) was one of the Atlanteans taken over by Stagecoach. Renumbered 1200 and repainted in Stagecoach livery with Ribble fleetnames, it is seen in Fishergate, Preston on 18th May 1994. *(BD)*

Right. Local identity was restored in February 1997 when Cumberland took over and the name 'Stagecoach Lancaster' was used in conjunction with Cumberland legal lettering. *(HP)*

APPENDIX 1 - THE TRAM FLEETS

Note that the seating of double-deck cars gives top deck first, to keep in line with bus fleet lists.

1. MORECAMBE TRAMWAYS COMPANY (1887-1924)

Year in Service	Fleet Nos.	Builder	Type	Seats	Power	Notes
1887	1-2	Lancaster RC&W	Open top d/d	23/18	Horse-drawn	
1887	3-4	Lancaster RC&W	Toast rack	29	Horse-drawn	
1888	5-6	Lancaster RC&W	Open top d/d	24/20	Horse-drawn	
1889	7	Lancaster RC&W	Open top d/d	24/20	Horse-drawn	
1897	8-11	Lancaster RC&W	Open top d/d	26/22	Horse-drawn	
c.1898	12-15	??	Open top d/d	??	Horse-drawn	1
1901	16-17	??	Open top d/d	??	Horse-drawn	
1912	1-3	UEC/Leyland	Covered s/d	35	55 hp petrol	
1913	4	UEC/Leyland do	Open s/d	35	55 hp petrol	

1 Smaller than the earlier double-deckers, possibly second-hand.

2. LANCASTER & DISTRICT TRAMWAYS COMPANY (1890–1921)

1890	1-14??	Lancaster RC&W	Open top d/d	22/18	Horse-drawn	2

2 Some cars later altered to open higher-floored single deck by lowering the top deck to waist level.

3. LANCASTER CORPORATION (1903-1930)

Year in Service	Fleet Nos.	Builder	Type	Seats	Power	Notes
1903	1-10	Lancaster RC&W	Open top d/d Reversed Staircases	23/18	Brill 21	3; 4
1905	11-12	Milnes Voss	Open top d/d Direct staircases	23/18	M&G 21EM	3; 4

3 Balcony top covers fitted in 1911/2 by Milnes Voss (four) and in 1913/4 by UEC (two). 2, 3, 6-9 confirmed as fitted, four cars remained open top.
4 Eight cars (1, 2, 4, 5, 9-12) were rebuilt starting in 1917 to totally enclosed single deck 24 seats, one-man operated. The process was spread through until c1923.

4. MORECAMBE CORPORATION (1909-1926)

Year in Service	Fleet Nos.	Builder	Type	Seats	Power	Notes
1909	(twelve)	Misc	Open top d/d	varied	Horse-drawn	5
1909	(two)	Lancaster RC&W	Toast Rack	29	Horse-drawn	5
1919	14, 15	English Electric	Toast Rack	32	Horse-drawn	
1922	(one)	Lancaster RC&W	Open top d/d	22/18	Horse-drawn	6
1922	13, 16	English Electric	Open top d/d	22/18	Horse-drawn	

5 Purchased with Morecambe part of Morecambe Tramways Co system in July 1909. There was probably some renumbering involving a few cars then, making numbering unclear.
6 Acquired from Lancaster & District Tramways Co in January 1922.

APPENDIX 2 - LANCASTER CORPORATION BUS FLEET

Year	Reg. Nos.	Fleet Nos.	Chassis	Body and seating	Notes
1916	B 5981/79	1-2	Edison Battery	Brush B22F	
1917	B 5982	3	Edison Battery	Brush B22F	
1918	B 5998/34	4-5	Edison Battery	J A Hardy B25F	
1925	TD 1587	6	Daimler CKA	Buckingham B24F	
1925	TD 4147	7	Overland BMT	Barton Townley B14F	
1926	TD 4921	8	Daimler CM	Buckingham B32F	
1927	TD 8695	9	Daimler CKA	Buckingham B24F	
1928	TE 3333/5684	10,12	Leyland PLC1	Leyland B26F	
1928	TE 4079	11	ADC 424	G. Fox B26F	
1929	TE 7981	13	Leyland PLC1	Leyland B26F	
1929	TE 8119-21	14,?, 15	Daimler CF6	NCME B26F	
1930	TF 200-3	16,?,17,18	Daimler CF6	NCME B26F	
1930	TF 694-7	19,?, ? 21	Daimler CF6	NCME B26F	
1931	TF 4032	?	Daimler CF6	NCME B26F	1
1931	TF 6483	?	Daimler CH6	Weymann B32F	
1932	VC 5722/9147	??	Daimler CF6	Buckingham B32F	1
1932	XJ 282	?	Daimler CP6	Burlingham H28/24R	1 2
1932	TF 9646	23	AEC Regent	English Electric H28/24R	3

Year	Registration	Fleet No	Chassis	Body	Notes
1932	MV 1518	?	AEC Regent	Brush H30/26R	3 4
1934	TJ 6559/60	1,2	Crossley Condor	Crossley H24/24R	
1936	ATF 556/7	6,7	Daimler COG5	English Electric H26/22R	
1936	ATF 558/9	26,27	Daimler COG5/40	English Electric B39R	
1937	CTB 641/2	8,9	Daimler COG5	English Electric H26/22R	
1937	CTB 643/4	28,29	Daimler COG5/40	English Electric B39R	
1938	CTF 881-3	30-32	Daimler COG5/40	English Electric B39R	
1938	CTF 884	33	Daimler COG5	English Electric H26/22R	
1939	DTE 918	34	Daimler COG5	Willowbrook H22/26R	
1939	DTE 919/20	35,36	Daimler COG5	Willowbrook B32R	
1940	ETE 381	39	Daimler COG5	Willowbrook H22/26R	
1940	ETE 382/3	37,38	Daimler COG5	Willowbrook B32R	
1941	FTB 299	40	TSM H5LA4	Willowbrook B26F	5
1942	FTB 298	41	Leyland TD7	East Lancs H30/26R	
1942	FTC 317	42	Guy Arab I 5LW	Brush H30/26R	6
1943	FTD 69	43	Guy Arab I 5LW	Pickering H30/26R	6
1943	FTD 70	44	Daimler CWG5	Massey H30/26R	7
1943	FTD 726/7	45,46	Guy Arab II 5LW	Pickering H30/26R	6
1944	FTE 66/7	47,48	Guy Arab II 5LW	Massey H30/26R	7
1944	FTE 181/2	49,50	Guy Arab II 5LW	Massey H30/26R	7
1947	HTB 442/3	442/3	Leyland PS1	Crossley B36R	
1947	HTB 444-7	444-7	Crossley DD42/3T	Crossley H30/26R	8
1947	HTC 613-5	613-5	Crossley SD42/3	Crossley B36R	
1947	HTF 569-72	569-72	Crossley DD42/3	Crossley H30/26R	
1948	JTD 961-5	961-5	Crossley DD42/3	Crossley H30/26R	
1951	NTC 708-10	708-0	Leyland PD2/1	Leyland H30/26R	
1953	NTF 466-8	466-8	Daimler CVG5	NCME B36R	
1953	KTF 581/2	581/2	AEC Regal	Strachans B36F	9
1953	GYE 97	97	Guy Arab II 5LW	Park Royal H30/26R	10
1953	GYL 459	459	Guy Arab II 5LW	Park Royal H30/26R	10
1953	HGC 105	105	Guy Arab II 5LW	Park Royal H30/26R	10
1953	HGC 174	174	Guy Arab II5LW	Weymann H30/26R	10
1957	881/2 BTF	881/2	Leyland PD2/41	East Lancs H35/28R	
1957	128/9 DTD	128/9	Leyland PD2/41	East Lancs H35/28R	
1957	JDK 711/3-5	711/13-5	AEC Regal IV	Burlingham B44F	11
1958	175-7 FTJ	175-7	Leyland PSUC1/3	East Lancs B43F	
1959	389/90 JTD	389/90	Leyland PSUC1/3	East Lancs B43F	
1961/2	101-3 UTF	101-3	Leyland L1	East Lancs B42D	
1963	201-3 YTE	201-3	Leyland PD2/37	East Lancs H37/28F	
1965	KTJ 204-6C	204-6	Leyland PD2/37	East Lancs H37/28F	
1967/8	GTC 104-6F	104-6	Leyland PSUR1/1R	East Lancs B53F	
1968	LTC 107-9F	107-9	Leyland PSUR1/1R	East Lancs B53F	
1969	RTE 110-2G	110-12	Leyland PSU3A/2R	East Lancs B51F	
1970	YTE 113-5H	113-5	Leyland PSU3A/2R	East Lancs B51F	
1972	NTD 116-8K	116-8	Leyland PSU3B/2R	Seddon B51F	
1972	STD 119-2L	119-21	Leyland PSU4B/2R	Seddon B47F	
1973/4	PTC 122-4M	122-4	Leyland National 1051/1R	Leyland. National B41F	

Notes.

1 Ex-Daimler, Coventry

2 Converted to CH6 standard according to a Department list, by late 1937

3 Fitted with AEC A162 diesel engine in 1935. Seating of TF 9646 then became H24/24

4 Ex AEC, Southall

5 Built for China Omnibus 1942

6 Rebodied Park Royal/Guy H30/26R in 1952

7 Rebodied Crossley H30/26R in 1950 (70,181) and 1951 (66 67,182)

8 Original Brockhouse turbo-transmission replaced by standard gearbox 1954/5

9 Ex-Morecambe and Heysham

10 Ex-London Transport

11 Ex-Rochdale

APPENDIX 3 - MORECAMBE & HEYSHAM BUS FLEET

Year	Reg. Nos.	Fleet Nos.	Chassis	Body and seating	Notes
1919	B 8704/5	1/2	Tilling Stevens TS3	Brush B30F	
1920	TB 2557	L1	Leyland G	Leyland O20/23RO	
1921	TB 6398	L2	Leyland G	Leyland O20/??RO	
1925	TD 2267/8	G1/3	Guy BB	Guy B30R	1
1925	TD 2715	G22	Guy BB	Guy B30R	
1926	TD 5446/7	G4/5	Guy BB	Guy B30D	
1926	TD 7098/7135	G6/7	Guy FBX	Short O53RO	
1926	TD 7205/6	G8/9	Guy FBX	Short O53RO	
1926	TD 7299/300	G10/11	Guy FBX	Short O53RO	
1927	TD 9800/01	G12/3	Guy BB	Guy B38T	2
1928	TE 2718/9	G14/5	Guy FBX	Short O53RO	3
1928	TE 4149	M16	Maudslay ML3	Hall Lewis B32D	
1928	TE 4303	D17	Dennis E	Hall Lewis B32D	
1928	TE 5064	D18	Dennis G	J A Cross B20F	
1928	TE 5485	D19	Dennis G	J A Cross B20F	
1929	TE 8044/5	20/1	Maudslay ML3B	Hall Lewis B32D	
1929	TE 9035/6	22/3	Dennis G	JA Cross B20F	
1929	TE 9281/2	24/5	Dennis G	JA Cross B20F	
	TE 8766	28	Karrrier JH	? B29D	4
	TD 866	26	AEC 504	LGOC O52RO	4
	TD 1921	30?	Overland	Warwick B14F	4
	TD 5009	31?	Overland BMT	Widdison B13F	4
	TD 5314	27	Karrier KL	? O28/26RO	4
	TD 6291	32?	Overland BMT	Widdison B14F	4
	TD 6665	33?	Overland BMT	Widdison B14F	4
1930	TF 2028	29	Maudslay ML3BC	NCME B32D	5
1932	TF 7464	1	AEC Regal	Weymann B32R	
1932	TF 7465-70	28/30-4	AEC Regent	Weymann H30/26R	
1933	TJ 2490-2	35-7	AEC Regent	Weymann H30/26R	
1934	TJ 5788/9	12/3	AEC Regent	Weymann H30/26R	
1935	TJ 9602/3	38/9	AEC Regent	Park Royal H30/26R	
1935	TJ 9822-5	2-5	AEC Regent	Weymann./Park Royal H30/26R	6
1936	ATF 994/5	11/27	AEC Regent	Park Royal H30/26R	
1936	ATJ 588/9	40/1	AEC Regent	Park Royal H28/28R	7
1937	BTF 234-9	6/9/26/42-4	AEC Regent	Park Royal H28/28R	6 7
1938	CTF 861	45	AEC Regent	Park Royal H28/28R	5 7
1938	DTB 61-4	16/7/24/5	AEC Regent	Park Royal H28/28R	6 7 8
1938	DTB 65-70	46-51	AEC Regent	Park Royal H28/28R	8
1947	GTJ 691-6	1/7/8/10/4/5	AEC Regent II	Park Royal H30/26R	
1948	JTE 544-9	18-23	AEC Regent III	Park Royal H30/26R	
1949	KTF 583-94	54-65	AEC Regent III	Park Royal H30/26R	9
1950	KTF 581/2	52/3	AEC Regal III	Strachans B35F	
1950	LTF 251-6	66-71	AEC Regent III	Park Royal H30/26R	
1950	MTC 540	72	AEC Regent III	Park Royal H30/26R	5
1951	MTE 635-40	73-8	AEC Regent III	Weymann H30/26R	
1954	TTB 688-90	79-81	AEC Regent III	Park Royal H30/26R	
1956	791/2 ATD	82/3	AEC Regent V	Massey H30/26R	
1957	793-5 ATD	84/6	AEC Regent V	Massey H30/26R	10
1960	33-5 MTD	87/9	Leyland PD2/37	Massey H37/27F	
1962	435/6 XTF	90/1	Leyland PD2A/27	Massey H37/27F	
1967	CTJ 101-6E	1-6	AEC Swift	Pennine B50D	
1968	HTJ 377F	7	AEC Swift	Pennine B50D	
1970	UTJ 908-10H	8-10	AEC Swift	NCME B50D	
1972	MTE 611-4K	11-4	Seddon RU 6HLX	Seddon B46D	11
1973	NTF 715/6M	15/6	Seddon RU 6HLX	Seddon DP47F	

Notes

1 G3 was B30D

2 G12/3 were toastracks

3 4 cylinder engines replaced by 6 cylinder later in 1928, upseated to 59

4 Ex-Heysham & District

5 Show exhibit

6 2 and 4 of 1935 fitted with AEC 7.7 diesel engines in 1945, refitted to 26 and 44 of 1937 in 1951/2 and again refitted to 25 and 49 of 1938 in 1956/7

7 Delivered with 'Sunsaloon' sliding roof sections, permanently panelled over during the war

8 25 and 49 converted to O28/28R in 1962

9 60-5 converted to O33/26R in 1967/8 58 followed in 1970

10 84 was H30/26RD

11 13/4 were DP47F

APPENDIX 4 – LANCASTER CITY TRANSPORT FLEET 1974

Buses transferred in

Year	Reg. Nos.	Fleet Nos.	Chassis	Body and seating	Notes
From Lancaster Corporation					
1952	NTF 466	466	Daimler CVG5	NCME B35F	
1957	881 BTF	881	Leyland PD2/41	East Lancs H35/28R	
1957	128/9 DTD	128/9	Leyland PD2/41	East Lancs H35/28R	
1958	175 FTJ	175	Leyland PSUC1/3	East Lancs B43F	
1959	389/90 JTD	389/90	Leyland PSUC1/3	East Lancs B43F	
1961	101 UTF	101	Leyland L1	East Lancs B42D	
1962	102/3 UTF	102/3	Leyland L1	East Lancs B42D	
1963	201-3 YTE	201-3	Leyland PD2/37	East Lancs H37/28F	1
1965	KTJ 204-6C	204-6	Leyland PD2/37	East Lancs H37/28F	
1967	GTC 104/5F	104/5	Leyland PSUR1/1	East Lancs B53F	
1968	GTC 106F	106	Leyland PSUR1/1	East Lancs B53F	
1968	LTC 107-9F	107-9	Leyland PSUR1/1	East Lancs B53F	
1969	RTE 110-2G	110-2	Leyland PSU3A/2R	East Lancs B51F	
1970	YTE 113-5H	113-5	Leyland PSU3A/2R	East Lancs B51F	
1972	NTD 116-8K	116-8	Leyland PSU3B/2R	Seddon B51F	
1972	STD 119-2L	119-21	Leyland PSU4B/2R	Seddon B47F	
1972/3	PTC 122-4M	122-4	Leyland National 1051/1R	Leyland National B41F	
From Morecambe and Heysham Corporation					
1949	KTF 583-6/8	54-7/9	AEC Regent III	Park Royal H33/26R	
1949	KTF 587/9-94	58/60-5	AEC Regent III	Park Royal H33/26R	2
1950	LTF 251-4	66-9	AEC Regent III	Park Royal H33/26R	
1950	MTC 540	72	AEC Regent III	Park Royal H33/26R	
1951	MTE 635/8-40	73/6-8	AEC Regent III	Weymann H33/26R	
1954	TTB 688-90	79-81	AEC Regent III	Park Royal H33/26R	
1956	791/2 ATD	82/3	AEC Regent V	Massey H33/26R	
1957	793 ATD	84	AEC Regent V	Massey H33/26RD	
1957	794/5 ATD	85/6	AEC Regent V	Massey H33/26R	
1960	33-5 MTD	87-9	Leyland PD2/37	Massey H37/27F	1 2
1962	35/6 XTF	90/1	Leyland PD2A/27	Massey H37/27F	
1967	CTJ 101-6E	1-6	AEC Swift	Pennine B50D	
1968	HTJ 377F	7	AEC Swift	Pennine B50D	2
1970	UTJ 908-10H	8-10	AEC Swift	NCME B50D	2
1972	MTE 611-4K	11-4	Seddon RU 6HLX	Seddon DP47F	3
1973	NTF 715/6M	15/6	Seddon RU 6HLX	Seddon DP47F	

Notes

1 201-3 and 88 were converted to open-top in 1976/8

2 8-10,58,60/2/5 and 88 were renumbered in 1977 to match their registration numbers, Lancaster style, 88 at the time of its conversion to open-top. 7 was renumbered similarly in 1978

3 11,12 were B46D

Liveries:-

Of the ex-Lancaster vehicles, 128 and 881 retained the former Lancaster livery until withdrawn

Of the ex-Morecambe and Heysham vehicles, 54-57/9/61/3/4/7-9/72/7-86 retained the former MHCT livery until withdrawn

APPENDIX 5 – LANCASTER CITY COUNCIL FLEET
Purchases 1974-1986

Vehicles acquired at the formation are listed in Appendix 4.
The year column indicates the year into service at Lancaster.

Year	Reg. Nos.	F/Nos.	Chassis	Body and seating	Notes
1974	HHG 32/3	32/3	Leyland PD3/6	East Lancs H41/32F	1
1974	LHG 534-7	534-7	Leyland PD3/6	East Lancs H41/32F	1
1975	TBU 598G	598	Leyland PD3/4	East Lancs H41/32RD	3
1975	998 AKT	998	Leyland PD2/30	Massey H33/28R	4
1975	410/1 DKM	410/1	Leyland PD2/30	Massey H33/28R	4
1975	413 GKT	413	Leyland PD2/30	Massey H33/28R	4
1976	MFR 17/8P	17/8	Leyland PSU3C/2R	Alexander C49F	
1976	MFR 41/2P	41/2	Leyland PSU4C/2R	Alexander C41F	5
1976	MFR 125/6P	125/6	Leyland PSU4C/2R	Alexander B45F	
1976	MFR 301-6P	301-6	Leyland PSU3C/2R	Alexander B53F	
1977	WCW 307-14R	307-14	Leyland PSU3D/2R	Alexander B53F	
1977	WCW 315-8R	315-8	Leyland PSU3D/2R	Alexander DP49F	
1977	WFV 19/20R	19/20	Leyland PSU3E/2R	Alexander C49F	6
1978	ORC 768	768	Leyland PDR1/1	Weymann L39/34F	7
1978	VUB 398/400H	398/400	Leyland PSU3A/4R	Plaxton C53F	8
1978	DBA 212/3/5/7/8/27/8C	212 etc	Leyland PDR1/1	Met Camm H43/33F	6 9
1979	DBA 214/6C	214/6	Leyland PDR1/1	Met Camm H43/33F	9
1979	NCW 151/2T	151/2	Leyland PSU3E/2R	Duple B55F	
1979	URN 11/2V	11/2	Leyland PSU3E/2R	Duple C51F	5
1979	URN 153V	153	Leyland PSU3E/2R	Duple B55F	
1979	URN 207-9V	207-9	Leyland AN68A/2R	East Lancs H45/33F	
1980	DBA 230C	230	Leyland PDR1/1	Met Camm O43/33F	9
1980	DHG 210/1W	210/1	Leyland AN68A/2R	East Lancs H45/33F	
1981	MRJ 300F	300	Leyland PDR1/1	Met Camm H43/33F	9
1981	KCK 201-4W	201-4	Leyland AN68C/2R	East Lancs H50/36F	
1981	LFV 205/6X	205/6	Leyland AN68C/2R	East Lancs H50/36F	
1982	TCK 200/12X	200/12	Leyland AN68D/2R	East Lancs H50/36F	
1982	WCK 213/5Y	213/5	Leyland AN68D/2R	East Lancs H50/36F	
1983	JTE 546	20	AEC Regent III	Park Royal H33/26R	10
1983	BFV 221/2Y	221/2	Leyland AN68D/2R	East Lancs CH45/32F	
1984	A214 MCK	214	Leyland AN68D/2R	East Lancs H50/36F	11
1984	A223 MCK	223	Leyland AN68D/2R	East Lancs CH45/32F	
1984	PCW 511X	511	Ford Transit	Chesh Conv M12	12
1985	B99 YRN	99	Leyland TRCTL11	Duple C57F	
1985	UBV 85/7L	85/7	Leyland AN68/1R	East Lancs O45/31F	13
1985	UBV 89L	89	Leyland AN68/1R	East Lancs H45/31F	13
1986	UBV 84L	84	Leyland AN68/1R	East Lancs O45/31F	13
1986	C90 MHG	90	Leyland TRCTL11	Plaxton C53F	
1986	D98 SCW	98	Leyland TRCTL11	Duple C57F	

Notes
1 Ex-Burnley and Pendle
2 Ex-Midland Red
3 Ex-Merthyr Tydfil
4 Ex-Maidstone
5 41 re-seated to B45F in 1979, 11/2 became C53F in 1982
6 20 became 20R in 1983; 213 became 213C in 1982
7 Ex-Trent
8 Ex-Fishwick
9 Ex-Greater Manchester PTE. 218/27/8 rebuilt to O43/33F in 1981/80/79 respectively
10 Ex-Lancaster Corporation Publicity Department. Originally Morecambe and Heysham
11 214 had a split-step entrance
12 Ex-Lowton, Sunniside.
13 Ex-Blackburn

The ex-Maidstone PD2s never carried LCCPT livery. A number of other acquisitions operated initially in livery of the previous operator prior to repaint.
Regent 20 was restored to original MHCT livery.

APPENDIX 6 - LANCASTER CITY TRANSPORT Ltd FLEET LIST

Including LONSDALE COACHES Ltd

The following buses were taken over from Lancaster City Council on 26th October 1986.
For details see Appendix 5.

11/2/9, 20R, 20 (Regent), 42, 84/5/7/9, 90/8/9 *, 151-3, 200-15/21-3, 301/5-18, 511 (* See notes 7, 8)

In the lists below, the year column indicates <u>the year into service</u> at Lancaster.
Fleet numbers are only shown here in instances where actually carried.

Year	Reg. Nos.	F/Nos.	Chassis	Body and seating	Notes
1986	D154 THG	154	Leyland TRBTL	East Lancs B55F	1
1987	SEL 242/5-9H	242, etc	Leyland PDR1A/1	Alexander H43/31F	2
1987	URN 217R	217	Leyland PSU5A/4R	Duple C51F	3
1987	NRG 155/8/60-4M	155, etc	Leyland AN68/1R	Alexander H45/36F	4
1988	PRA 108-12R	108-12	Leyland PSU3C/4R	Alexander C49F	5
1988	AEF 91A	91	Leyland PSU3D/4R	Willowbrook C47F	6
1988	PRX 187B		Leyland PD3/4	NCME FCO39/30F	7 9
1988	GHN 857/8N	357/8	Bedford YRQ	Duple B36F	8
1988	HPY 364/5N	364/5	Bedford YRQ	Duple DP36F	8
1988	PRD 34		AEC Reliance	Plaxton C51F	9
1988	SRC 45L		Leyland PSU4B/4R	Plaxton C40F	9
1988	CUF 144/6/50/2L		Leyland AN68/1R	Willowbrook H44/29D	9
1988	XTF 811L		Leyland PSU3B/4R	Duple C49F	9
1988	GGG 310N		Leyland AN68/1R	Alexander H45/31F	9
1988	JGA 184N		Leyland AN68/1R	Alexander H45/31F	9
1988	GOG 684N		Bristol VRTSL6G	MCW H45/31F	9
1988	OCW 453P		Bristol RESL6G	East Lancs DP42F	9
1988	PYG 141R		Bedford YLQ	Plaxton C45F	9
1988	REK 923R		AEC Reliance	Duple C57F	9
1988	TWH 686T		Leyland PSU3E/4R	Plaxton C51F	9
1988	ANA 1/2T		Leyland PSU5C/4R	Duple C55F C52F (2)	9
1988	ANA 4T		Leyland PSU3E/4R	Duple C51F	9
1988	ANA 8T		AEC Reliance	Plaxton C53F	9
1988	BTO 291T		Bedford VAS5	Plaxton C29F	9
1988	TRN 801V		Ford Transit	Dormobile B16F	9
1988	MNC 501W		Leyland PSU5D/5R	Duple C50F	9
1988	OTB 130W		Ford Transit	Steedrive DP16F	9
1988	SND 84X		Leyland PSU3B/4R	Duple C51F	9
1988	HFM 832X		Fiat 35-8	Reeve Burgess M12	9
1988	PRA 113-5R	113-5	Leyland PSU3C/4R	Alexander C49F	5
1988	JGA 190N		Leyland AN68/1R	Alexander H45/31F	10
1988	JUS 790N		Leyland AN68/1R	Alexander H45/31F	10
1988/9	HPY 317/8N	M17/8	Ford A0609	NCME DP20F	8
1989	EYH 807V	807	Leyland PSU3E/4R	Duple C49F	11
1989	NRG 165/7-70M	165, etc	Leyland AN68/1R	Alexander H45/36F	12
1989	MFR 17P	17	Leyland PSU3C/2R	Alexander C49F	13
1989	B118 RRE	Ford Transit	Ford Transit	Dormobile-PMT B16F	9 14
1989	XCC 295V	295	Ford AO609	Moseley B29F	
1989	D939 KNW	239	VW LT55	Optare B25F	16
1989	D231 TBW	231	VW LT55	Optare B25F	16
1989	E234-6 VUD	234-6	VW LT55	Optare B25F	16
1989	D81 NWW		VW LT55	Optare B25F	9 17
1990	E209/13/6 PWY	M2-4	VW LT55	Optare B25F	18
1990	A203 OCW		Leyland TRCTL11	Plaxton C53F	19
1990	C913 XEO		Leyland TRCTL11	Duple C53F	20
1990	E404 BHK	M11	VW LT55	Optare B25F	21
1990/1	WRJ 447/8X	447/8	Volvo-Ailsa B55	NCME H43/35F	22
1991	NNA 134W	446	Volvo-Ailsa B55	NCME H44/35F	22
1991	F414 KHR	M14	VW LT55	Optare B25F	23
1991	E212 PWY	M12	VW LT55	Optare B23F	24
1991	B59 AOP	M13	Ford Transit	Carlyle B16F	25
1991	A620/1 ATV		Leyland TRCTL11	Plaxton C53F	9 26

1991	B926 DTU	M15	Mercedes L608D	PMT C21F	27
1991	E403 BHK	M16	VW LT55	Optare B25F	28
1991	WAO 644Y	644	Leyland TRCTL/11	Alexander C47F	29
1991	UKE 827X	827	Leyland PSU3G/4R	ECW C49F	30
1992	H840 UUA	M17	Optare MR09	Optare B23F	31
1992	UKE 829X		Leyland PSU3G/4R	ECW C38FL	30
1992	D120 GWS		Leyland TRCTL/11	Plaxton C53F	9 32
1992	C76 KLG		Leyland TRCTL/11	Duple C49FT	9 33
1992	C854 VRY		MAN MT8.136	GC Smith C28F	34
1992	B902 DTU	M18	Mercedes L608D	PMT C21F	35
1992	K100 LCT	ML1	Optare MR01	Optare DP31F	
1992	K200/300 LCT	ML2/3	Optare MR01	Optare B31F	36
1992	J363 BNW	M19	Optare MR09	Optare B23F	31
1993	D457 EEG	C12	Leyland Royal Tiger	Leyland C53F	9 37
1993	J366 BNW	ML4	Optare MR03	Optare B29F	

Notes

1 Lancaster City Council order

2 Ex-Bournemouth

3 Ex-Ribble. Later in 1987, 217 became AEF 88A and was re-numbered 88

4 Ex-Fife Scottish

5 Ex-Trent

6 Ex-Wessex National. AEF 91A was re-registered from SAD 124R before entering service

7 Ex-Southdown

8 Ex-Cleveland Transit

9 Ex-Lonsdale Coaches. SRC 45L was originally HPJ 999K. D81 NWW and B118 RRE were numbered M1 and M10 respectively in 1990. PRX 187B numbered 187 in 1991; TWH 686T numbered 686 in 1992. SND 84X had a 1975 chassis re-bodied and re-registered in 1982. In 1990, 90/8/9 lost their fleet numbers on repainting in the revised Lonsdale livery. In 1992 the Lonsdale coach fleet was numbered and many were re-registered as follows; C76 KLG became HIL 8914, numbered C14; D120 GWS became HIL 8915, numbered C15; C90 MHG became IIL 2490, numbered C90; D98 SCW became IIL 3198, numbered C98; B99 YRN numbered C99. A620/1 ATV numbered C20/1, but later that year transferred to LCT and re-numbered 620/1. In 1993 D457 EEG became IIL 4012

10 Ex-Peter, Sheffield

11 Ex-Burton, Brixham

12 Ex-Highland Scottish

13 Re-acquired after six years at Eastbourne 14 Ex-PMT

15 Ex-Morris, Ebbw Vale

16 Ex-Thames Transit. 231/4-6/9 re-numbered M5-9 respectively in 1990

17 Ex-Devon General

18 Ex-BTS, Borehamwood

19 Ex-Robinson, Great Harwood

20 Ex-Barrow, later numbered C13

21 Ex-Derby

22 Ex-GM Buses

23 Ex-MAN-VW, Swindon

24 Ex-Tayside. M12 was quickly up-seated to B25F. C99 reverted to C57F in 1993

25 Ex-West Midlands Travel

26 Ex-Hyndburn

27 Ex-Annis, Felling

28 Ex-Burman, Mile Oak

29 Ex Portsmouth Transit

30 Ex-East Kent. UKE 829X became C16 HIL 8916 and A203 OCW became C17 HIL 8917

31 Ex-Demonstrator

32 Ex-Blue Iris, Nailsea

33 Ex-Goldline, Nottingham

34 Ex-Peterborough Taxis. C854 VRY became HIL 9311, numbered C11

35 Ex-Philjo, Telford

36 ML2/3 re-registered K450/49 YCW respectively in 1993

37 Ex-Horrocks, Brockton

LIVERY NOTES

LCT fleet

The restored Morecambe & Heysham Regent (20) remained in MHCT colours. Overall adverts (applied when with LCCPTD) lasted until 1987 on 212 (Thwaites Bitter) or 1989 on 151 (Solid Fuel Advisory Service) and 316 (John O' Gaunt Tickets).

A number of acquisitions operated initially in liveries of their previous operators prior to repaint, but JGA 190N, JUS 790N and ML4 operated only in 'as acquired' liveries. PRX 187B ran in traditional Southdown colours until the 1991 fleet livery repaint when it was numbered.

There were several variations in fleet livery, but basically what was initially an amended LCCPT livery was revised in 1990, using new shades of blue in revised styling. A coach version introduced then was mainly white using blue stripes. 91/9 and 217 carried National Express livery 1987/8.

The livery of the first VW LT55's as acquired was adopted for later vehicles of this type. M17 (H840 UUA) was painted black and gold before use, branded for 'Unisprint' service. ML2 was painted from new in advertising livery for IPC Insurances. ML3 was painted from new in advertising livery for Farrell Heyworth & Jackson's. M19 was painted before use in advertising livery for Concept uPVC Windows & Doors. M3 was repainted 1993 in advertising livery for Weatherwarm Windows. M16 was repainted 1993 in advertising livery for Plas-Tech Windows.

Lonsdale Coaches Fleet

No immediate livery change was made after this 1988 acquisition. Most double decks (and their later replacements) carried special liveries, viz:- Isle of Man Steam Packet Co: CUF 144/6/50/2L. Later Isle of Man Seaways: 165/9/70, Pontin's: JGA 184N and 167, Asda: GOG 684N and 168. 165/7-70 had these special liveries applied before use. In 1990 the coach fleet received an updated livery of white with red, yellow and blue stripes, similar in style to the revised LCT coach livery.

Fleet ownership and transfers

Numerous loans between the fleets occurred, but only changes of fleetname are recorded here.

TWH 686T was transferred to the LCT fleet in 1990, the only original Lonsdale vehicle to transfer. Several later acquisitions went directly into the Lonsdale fleet, viz: 165/7-70, M13/5, M18 (B902 DTU), XCC 295V, UKE 829X, A203 OCW, A620/1 ATV, B118 RRE, C76 KLG, C854 VRY, C913 XEO, D120 GWS and D457 EEG. Of these, A620/1 ATV were transferred to the LCT fleet in 1992. Some LCT vehicles were transferred to the Lonsdale fleet from the dates shown below:-

   1988: 98/9.
   1989: 12, 42, 90, 222 (but 42 and 222 transferred back to LCT in 1990).
   1990: M9 (transferred back to LCT later that year).
   1991: 155/60.

APPENDIX 7
LANCASTER, MORECAMBE and HEYSHAM BUS OPERATORS - EARLY NOTES
by Richard Allen

While these notes cannot claim to be exhaustive they should help to clarify developments during the early years of bus operation until the 1930 Road Traffic Act took effect.

To set the scene, in 1914 the four tramway systems in the area were at their maximum extent, and the joining together of Morecambe Borough with Heysham Urban District was still some years off.

Before the 1930 Act was implemented services, vehicles, drivers and conductors had to be licensed by the relevant local Watch Committee (usually renewable at the time of an annual inspection).

The Chief Constable would make recommendations regarding the location of terminal stands.

In Lancaster, Dalton Square was fixed as the terminal bus stand for new out-of-town services in 1921 until capacity was reached in 1928, after which newcomers were allocated a stand at Damside Street.

Lancaster service authorisations referred to were those of Lancaster Watch Committee, which always insisted on restrictions to protect the Corporation's own services.

Note that several operators listed also ran garage businesses and/or coach operations which may have continued after bus operations ceased.

Long-distance services, which started picking up in the district around 1928, are not covered here.

Please refer to the earlier text for other developments affecting the municipal and company tramway operators. Further notes follow this section regarding the development of company bus services in Morecambe and Heysham.

Operators listed appear in the order of earliest bus operation locally.

Lancaster & District Tramways Co

The first local bus operation in the district, from 9th April 1914, merely supplemented the tram route until the vehicles were commandeered for Military use on 18th September that year.

Lancaster & District Tramways Co and Fahy's Ltd (joint bus committee) (referred to as L&DT-Fahy's)

Bus operation restarted in January 1915, again over the tram route. Fahy's Ltd, local Leyland dealer and owner of Royal Red motor coaches since 1907, supplied vehicles on the basis of half L&DT-owned and half Fahy's-owned, with profits and maintenance costs shared equally. The tram service was then reduced to the minimum for keeping the company's rights intact until it ceased on the last day of 1921.

The service was extended to Heysham in September 1925.

Services introduced from Lancaster to Yealand and to Bare (Mayfield Garage).

Taken over 12th February 1926 by Lancashire & Westmorland Motor Services Ltd.

Lancaster Corporation

Bus operation began 30th November 1916. Market Square was established as terminal for Corporation bus operations as new services gradually developed, remaining so until the new Damside Street Bus Station opened in 1939. The last trams ran on 31st March 1930. All services ran within the Borough boundary before 1932.

Morecambe Corporation

Bus operation began 1st August 1919, supplementing the Promenade tram service, Battery - Bare.

Extension to Heysham (jointly worked with Morecambe Tramways Co) started 1st April 1924.

Further new services were developed.

Horse trams last ran on 4th October 1926, being replaced by pneumatic-tyred six-wheel double-deckers.

The Borough was merged with Heysham Urban District on 1st October 1928, to form the Borough of Morecambe & Heysham.

Lambsfield Bus Service (JT Atkinson), Skerton

Bus operation began February 1921 from Lancaster to Carnforth and Warton.

Reformed November 1922 as Lambsfield Motors Ltd (JT. Atkinson later re-started on his own).

Lancaster Engineering & Motor Co Ltd

Services authorised in June 1921 from Lancaster to Halton and also via Brookhouse to Hornby.

Service later started to Cockerham, extending to Knott End.

Licences transferred to County Motors, June 1923.

Garstang Motor Engineering Co Ltd

Garstang - Lancaster service authorised in July 1921.

Castle Motors Ltd took over operations in 1923.

Ex-Servicemen's Transport Co, Lancaster

Lancaster - Garstang service (one bus) authorised in February 1922.

Renamed County Motors (Lancaster) Ltd in May 1922.

A Robinson

Lancaster - Halton - Caton - Brookhouse service authorised in February 1922, subject to the vehicle being satisfactory. If begun, this appears to have ceased again by 1925.

County Motors (Lancaster) Ltd

This was previously Ex-Servicemen's Transport Co, being renamed in May 1922.

The principal shareholders were Morecambe Motors Ltd (who also ran Silver Grey motor coaches).

Took over buses of Galgate Motors (no previous reference), November 1922.

Licences of Lancaster Engineering & Motor Co Ltd transferred, June 1923.

Services developed to Kirkby Lonsdale, Morecambe, Heysham, Skipton and Preston.
Ribble Motor Services obtained controlling interest July 1928 resulting in co-ordination on competing routes.
Further services authorised Lancaster - Hest Bank and also to Halton.
Taken over by Ribble MS 1st February 1929, but retained as subsidiary thereof.
Fully absorbed by Ribble in December 1930.

Lambsfield Motors Ltd, Skerton

Reformed from J T Atkinson's Lambsfield Bus Service in November 1922.
Services developed Lancaster to Kellet, Kirkby Lonsdale, Morecambe (Tower), Priest Hutton, Kendal and Garstang.
Taken over 12th February 1926 by Lancashire & Westmorland Motor Services Ltd, including the garage which later became Ribble's Skerton depot.

Tourist Motors (LE Jenkinson), Heysham

Started in January 1923 with a Saturdays Overton - Lancaster service. With a seasonal charabanc sideline (as had most seaside garage proprietors then), for this service he used one of two former Thomas Tilling petrol-electric double-deckers.
Further developments took place as outlined in notes following this section.
Finally ceased bus operation in November 1924. Mr Jenkinson cited the reason as Heysham UDC's grant of only one bus licence, which he considered insufficient to run a reliable service.

Morecambe Tramways Co

Started bus operation March 1923, on the same Battery - Heysham route as Tourist Motors, to counter competition from the latter to the Company's petrol trams.
Extension of this to Bare (jointly worked with Morecambe Corporation) started on 1st April 1924.
Last day of petrol trams was 24th October 1924.
Service to Overton started 9th December 1924 (in place of former Tourist Motors operation).
Fleet and operations transferred to Heysham & District Motors Ltd, January 1925.

Castle Motors Ltd, Garstang

Formed in 1923 from Garstang Motor Engineering Co Ltd.
Garstang - Cockerham - Lancaster and also Lancaster - Abbeystead and Knott End services authorised.
Licences transferred July 1926 to The Pilot Motors, Preston (who were previously met at Garstang).

Heysham & District Motors Ltd

Commenced January 1925 by taking over fleet and operations of Morecambe Tramways Co.
Agreement of November 1926 for sale to Morecambe Corporation had to be shelved as latter did not at the time have the statutory powers to operate outside that Borough.
Business taken over by Morecambe & Heysham Corporation, 4th May 1929.

J T Atkinson, Skerton

Restarted operations independent from the Lambsfield concern in February 1925, with a Lancaster - Halton via Ramparts service.
Services later started to Warton, Kellet via Bolton le Sands, Hest Bank, and Arnside via Milnthorpe.
Taken over by Ribble MS on 1st February 1929.

Westmorland Motor Services, Whitehaven (associated with Cumberland MS, BAT. subsidiary)

Kendal - Endmoor - Burton - Lancaster service authorised in September 1925.
Reformed on 12th February 1926 as Lancashire & Westmorland Motor Services Ltd (the Cumberland MS interests then transferring to Ribble).

The Pilot Motors Ltd, Preston

Took over licences of Castle Motors, Garstang in July 1926.
Taken over by Ribble MS on 23rd October 1926.

Lancashire & Westmorland Motor Services Ltd, Lancaster (BAT subsidiary)

Reformed from Westmorland MS 12th February 1926, when L&DT-Fahy's, and Lambsfield Motors Ltd operations were also acquired.
Service later authorised Lancaster - Ingleton - Skipton.
In Lancaster the former L&DT-Fahy's stand in St Leonardgate (by Stonewell) transferred to Dalton Square in November 1927.
Absorbed by Ribble Motor Services Ltd on 13th December 1927.

Ribble Motor Services Ltd, Preston (BAT. subsidiary)

Lancaster to Preston and Blackpool services (to be run in conjunction with L&WMS) authorised in September 1926. This would have given Ribble their first foothold in Lancaster.
The Pilot Motors Ltd taken over on 23rd October 1926.
Lancashire & Westmorland Motor Services Ltd absorbed on 13th December 1927, boosting the local presence.
Lancaster - Skipton and Blackpool - Knott End - Lancaster - Ingleton services authorised in March 1928.
Controlling interest obtained July 1928 in County Motors (Lanc'r) Ltd, resulting in co-ordination on previously competing routes.
JT Atkinson and County Motors both taken over on 1st February 1929 (County Motors retained as a subsidiary).
Kendal Motor Bus Co taken over on 12th April 1930.
Castle Station - Glasson Dock service started 7th July 1930, following withdrawal of the rail passenger service from this branch line.
County Motors subsidiary fully absorbed in December 1930. The County Motors depot in Dalton Square was retained until a rebuilt Skerton depot was opened in 1934.
Co-ordinated service with Pennine MS arranged on Ingleton route from December 1930.

Kendal Motor Bus Co

Kendal - Lancaster service authorised in November 1927.

Taken over by Ribble MS on 12th April 1930.

Pennine Motor Services, Skipton (later Gargrave)

Skipton - Morecambe via Lancaster service authorised in September 1928 - but no stand allotted in Lancaster initially.

Allocated a Lancaster stand at Damside Street from November 1928 on the above service.

Co-ordinated service with Ribble MS arranged on Ingleton route in December 1930, when it was planned for Pennine to switch to the Dalton Square stand. However, this latter move had not happened by May 1931 and instead the whole service was later switched to Damside Street.

Morecambe & Heysham Corporation

Enlarged Borough formed on 1st October 1928, operations of former Morecambe Corporation continued.

Business of Heysham & District Motors taken over on 4th May 1929, which included the Overton service, although partly outside the Borough.

John Fawcett & Sons (t/a Dallam Motor Services), Milnthorpe

Arnside - Silverdale - Carnforth - Lancaster service authorised in October 1928.

This was the last new bus operator to appear in the area until 1986.

This was the first operator to be allocated a stand at Damside Street, Dalton Square having filled to capacity.

Notes on annual licences granted etc

July 1920   By Lancaster Watch Committee:-

Lancaster Corporation (5 electric buses and 12 electric tramcars),

L&DT including Fahy's (6 motor buses and 3 horse tramcars).

May 1925   Then licensed in area:-

Morecambe Corporation (4 + trams), Heysham & District (4), Lancaster Corporation (6 + trams),

L&DT-Fahy's (13), Lambsfield (17), County Motors (16), JT Atkinson (3), Castle Motors (6).

May 1926   By Lancaster Watch Committee (buses):-

Lancaster Corporation (8), L&WMS (44), County Motors (24), JT Atkinson (6), Castle Motors (6).

May 1928   By Lancaster Watch Committee (buses):-

Lancaster Corporation (10, various routes),

Ribble (352, routes to Preston, Knott End, Blackpool, Morecambe, Heysham, Kendal & north, Ingleton & Skipton, Quernmore. The full fleet appears to have been licensed here),

County Motors (25, routes to Knott End, Morecambe, Heysham, Kirkby Lonsdale, Ingleton),

Kendal Motor Bus Co (18, routes to Kendal, Halton),

JT Atkinson (6, routes to Warton, Halton).

In the 7-day period commencing 12th August 1928, a traffic census on Skerton Bridge recorded 11,331 buses.

This figure would have included all bus and coach traffic and not just local bus services.

By the end of 1930, in time for the implementing of the 1930 Road Traffic Act, the number of bus operators in the district had settled down to five - the two Corporations, Ribble, Dallam and Pennine. Dallam continued until taken over by Ribble in 1950, and Pennine would later retrench to North Yorkshire at deregulation in 1986.

APPENDIX 8
COMPANY BUS OPERATION IN MORECAMBE and HEYSHAM - EARLY CHRONOLOGY 1914-21
by Richard Allen

As recorded earlier the first bus operation in the district was that of Lancaster & District Tramways Co which started on 9th April 1914 supplementing their Lancaster - Morecambe tram service until it had to be discontinued when buses were commandeered on 18th September. The service resumed in January 1915 under the joint bus committee of Lancaster & District Tramways Co and Fahy's Ltd (henceforth referred to as L&DT-Fahy's). In Lancaster a stand in St Leonardgate was used, adjacent to their Stonewell tram terminus. The buses soon became the principal conveyance, and the tram service reduced to the minimum until abandoned on 31st December 1921. The tram replacement bus service was to continue to be free of restriction, regarding the carriage of local passengers, within the Borough between Torrisholme and the Town Centre.

1922
In May Morecambe Council had the terminal moved from Market Street to Queen Square.

1923
In January 'Tourist Motors' (LE Jenkinson) of Cumberland View, Heysham (also a charabanc proprietor) entered the scene with a Saturdays only Overton - Morecambe - Lancaster service. Heysham Council refused to license this, which meant that passengers could not board or alight between the boundaries at Middleton Road and the Battery.
In February, Heysham Council granted Tourist Motors one bus licence to operate another service, from the Battery to Higher Heysham (Smithy Lane) which ran outwards via Lower Heysham (Village Square) and School Road, but returned directly. This was allowed at a time when the Morecambe Tramways Co petrol tram service was curtailed at Four Lane Ends due to track works. For the foregoing he had obtained two ex- Thomas Tilling petrol-electric double-deckers.
In March, the Tramways Co retaliated by starting on the same route using an ex-Ribble Karrier double-decker (CK 3087).
In May, Heysham Council barred buses from Crimewell Lane (the hill into Lower Heysham), deeming it unsafe. Buses could still use Longlands Lane and School Road.
In August, Heysham Council at last authorised Tourist Motors Overton service. Now daily, it was combined with their Higher Heysham service, but it appears that the Lancaster Saturday extension was dropped.

1924
On 1st April through transport was re-established between Bare and Heysham after some 15 years of changing at the Battery, a joint service of Morecambe Corporation and Morecambe Tramways Co buses being started. The latter had obtained a second ex-Ribble Karrier and another bus in time for this. No reference was made at the time to Morecambe Corporation not having the powers to operate outside the Borough. Possibly a hiring arrangement was used to circumvent this. The revenue taken on all buses in Morecambe went to the Corporation and that taken in Heysham to the Company, separate tickets being issued.
On 18th June County Motors (Lancaster) Ltd started a service from Lancaster (Dalton Square) to Morecambe (West End Road/ Grove Street, adjacent to new Morecambe Motors garage), via Euston Grove. Trips alternated via the new Morecambe Road and Torrisholme village.
On 30th June Heysham Council refused to license Tourist Motors fleet and the service stopped. Two weeks later it was allowed to re-start, but using only one bus, a new Karrier 56-seater double-decker.
On 10th July, Lambsfield Motors Ltd started a new service from Morecambe (Lord Street, near the Tower) via 'the Morecambe Road extension' (later named Broadway), Torrisholme, Skerton, Carnforth, Warton and Beetham to Kendal.
On 24th October Morecambe Tramways Co petrol trams ceased operation.
In November, Tourist Motors finally ceased bus operation. The proprietor later cited the reason as Heysham Council only granting one bus licence, with which he could not run a reliable service.
On 9th December, Morecambe Tramways Co started a service to Overton in place of the former Tourist Motors operation.

1925
In about January, Morecambe Tramways Co bus fleet and operations were transferred to a new company, Heysham & District Motors Ltd.
Also in January, buses resumed running down Crimewell Lane into Lower Heysham village square.
In February, L&DT-Fahy's had a new service approved, from Lancaster via Bare Lane to Bare (Mayfield Garage).
In May, Heysham Council again stopped buses working down Crimewell Lane, due it seems to pressure from Morecambe Corporation. A solution soon resulted in Heysham & District operating to Lower Heysham (only), while Morecambe Corporation vehicles served Higher Heysham.
In September, an extension to County Motors' West End Road service was begun, via the Promenade and Heysham Road to the Strawberry (former Marine) Gardens at Heysham.
At the same time, L&DT-Fahy's began an extension of their Lancaster - Morecambe (Queen Square) former tram route, onward via Euston Grove, West End Road, Westminster Avenue, Westminster Road, Alexandra Road, and Heysham Road to Higher Heysham (Towers).
On both of these extensions, Morecambe Corporation was to receive receipts taken on the extended sections within the boundary and pick up arrangements in Heysham were restricted.
There were now four operators on Heysham Road.
In October, County Motors were authorised for a Lancaster - Morecambe (Queen Square) service.

1926
On 12th February, new operator Lancashire & Westmorland MS took over the operations of L&DT-Fahy's and also Lambsfield Motors Ltd locally, along with the L&DT depot at South Avenue.
On 1st March, County Motors started a service from Morecambe and Lancaster to Skipton.

In April a second joint operation between Morecambe Corporation and what was now Heysham & District Motors was authorised, from Euston Road Station via West End Road to Heysham.

On 6th November an agreement was made for Morecambe Corporation to purchase Heysham & District Motors, but had to be shelved pending the planned enlargement of the Borough as their were still no statutory powers to operate beyond the boundary. Also in November the long-established former L&DT-Fahy's (now L&WMS) stand at St Leonardgate, Lancaster was transferred to Dalton Square.

1927

On 13th December, Ribble Motor Services took over the operations of Lancashire & Westmorland MS.

1928

In July, Ribble obtained a controlling interest in County Motors (Lancaster) Ltd.

In August, Heysham Council refused to license Heysham & District's two solid-tyred double-deckers. Morecambe Corporation helped out by loaning their Leyland double-deckers (with solid tyres!).

In September, Pennine Motor Services were authorised to work a Morecambe - Lancaster - Skipton through service.

On 1st October Heysham Urban District was incorporated into the new Borough of Morecambe & Heysham. This allowed negotiations for the purchase of Heysham & District Motors to restart.

1929

On 1st February Ribble acquired County Motors, but it was retained as a subsidiary.

In March, an application by Heysham & District Motors to Lancaster Watch Committee for a Heysham to Lancaster service was rejected. This appears to have been a back-door attempt towards an inter-town municipal service.

On 4th May the Heysham & District business was duly taken over by Morecambe & Heysham Corporation. This included the Overton service, although partly outside the new Borough boundary.

1930

In May, Ribble and County Motors terminal point at Morecambe (Queen Square) was moved to the new Corporation Poulton Hall Bus Station (by the market). This was vacated six years later in favour of Ribble's new Euston Road Bus Station, after which the Poulton Hall site was used for coach parking.

In December the Ribble subsidiary of County Motors was fully absorbed.

This left just Ribble as the main company bus operator in Morecambe and Heysham, although Pennine Motors retained the odd working extending through to Morecambe right through until deregulation in 1986.

IN LOVING MEMORY OF MORECAMBE HORSE CARS. R.I.P.

In loving memory of Morecambe Horse Cars. This postcard was published to mark the passing of the horse trams. *(RA)*

ENGLANDS 1ST PETROL TRAM

In 1909 the Morecambe and District Tramways Company sold its Morecambe operations to the Corporation retaining only the short section of route in Heysham. In 1912 the company bought three petrol trams with Leyland engines on UEC frames and a further one the following year. The first tram ran on 15th January 1912, the service operating until 1924 when it was replaced by motor buses.

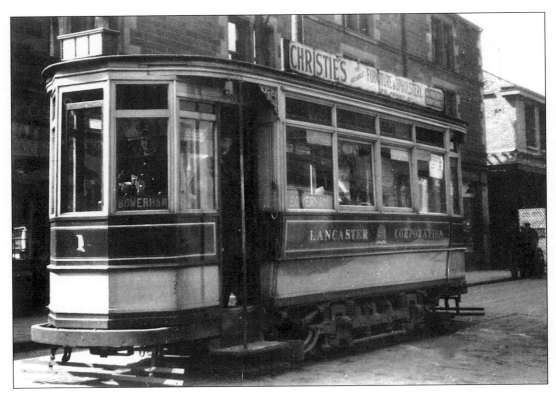

Above. Lancaster number 1, one of the six double-deck cars converted to single deck and known as 'coffins', is shown in the city centre ready to leave for Bowerham. *(STA/KIT)*

Middle. An unidentified coffin car at the Boot and Shoe terminus at Scotforth. Note the abbreviated LCT fleetname. *(LCT)*

Lower. A couple of interested onlookers get in the frame as the crew of number 12 pause for the photographer en route for Castle Railway Station. *(LCT)*

Lancaster's first buses arrived in 1916 and comprised two Edison battery-powered vehicles with 22-seat bodies by Brush. They were numbered 1 and 2 and number 1 (B 5981) is shown in the upper picture before entering service on the short route between the Market Square and the Caton projectile factory.

Number 3 (B 5982), seen in the middle view, arrived in the following year and was basically similar to its two predecessors although it had panels around the roof to carry advertising, in this case for The Valet Service of Church Street, Lancaster.

The final pair arrived in 1918 and carried 25-seat bodies by the local firm of J Hardy of Halton Road, Lancaster. In the lower picture number 5 (B 5934) stands with its crew in the Market Square. Note the unusual arrangement of the entrance. *(All LCT)*

Above. Andy Brew stands proudly at the front of number 8 (TD 4921), a Daimler CM with Buckingham body supplied in 1926. *(LCT)*

Below. Working the County Street to Sanatorium service is 1929 Daimler CF6 TE 8119, probably numbered 14, with body by the Northern Counties Motor and Engineering Company of Wigan. Standing at the front is Bill Parkinson who later became Chief Inspector. *(BPC)*

Above. Photographed when new in 1932 is number 23 (TF 9646), an AEC Regent with body by English Electric. In 1934 it was renumbered 5 and it was Lancaster's first double-decker. The body was reconditioned by East Lancashire Coachbuilders in 1942 and it was withdrawn in December 1945. *(LCT)*

Below. Number 26 (ATF 558) was one of two Daimler COG5 models with English Electric bodies purchased in 1936 and shown here when new. *(LCT)*

Above. Photographed when new is number 8 (CTB 641), a 1937 Daimler COG5 with body by English Electric. It was one of two supplied together with two single-deckers on the same chassis which marked the beginning of an association with the Daimler COG5 chassis which remained up to and including the final peace-time specifications in 1940. *(LCT)*

Below. Numbered 641 to coincide with its registration number in the 1946 renumbering scheme, number 8 was still going strong when photographed in Lancaster Bus Station in May 1952. It was withdrawn in May 1952. *(RM)*

Above. A solitary double-decker was purchased in 1940 along with two single-deckers, all on Daimler COG5 chassis and with bodies by Willowbrook. The double-decker 39 (ETE 381) is shown here. *(HPC)*

Below. DTE 920 was numbered 36 when delivered in 1939 but would receive the number 920 when the renumbering system was introduced after the war. It was a Willowbrook-bodied Daimler COG5. *(HPC)*

Above. This posed photograph shows Massey-bodied Guy Arab II number 47 (FTE 66) after repainting in standard fleet livery. *(RMC)*

Below. The first vehicle to wartime specification to arrive in the Lancaster fleet was number 42 (FTC 317) which came in September 1943. It is a Guy Arab I with bodywork by Brush. *(LCT)*

Above. Crossley number 570 (HTF 570) dating from 1947 emerges from Lancaster Bus Station on service 2 to Beaumont via Slyne Road. In the background is a Ribble half-cab coach showing Keswick as the destination. From close examination of the original photograph the service appears to be the X31 from Liverpool to Keswick. *(HPC)*

Below. Photographed in September 1968 when 17 years old is Leyland-bodied Leyland PD2 number 710 (NTC 710). *(RM)*

Upper. In 1957 four AEC Regal IV models with Burlingham bodies were purchased from Rochdale Corporation. The centre doors were removed by Burlingham and they were adapted for one-person operation before entering service. They were numbered 711/3-5 and were said to be thirsty vehicles. Number 711 (JDK 711) stands in the Bus Station in April 1958. *(RM)*

Middle. A further two East Lancs-bodied Leyland Tiger Cubs were purchased in 1949. Number 389 (389 JTD) is shown in the city centre. *(RM)*

Lower. The Leyland Panther with its rear engine and low entrance seemed an attractive proposition and three were delivered in 1967 followed by a further three in 1968. One of the 1968 batch is shown in Cable Street in June 1971. However, the Panther was not one of Leyland's more successful models and no further examples were purchased, a return being made to the well tried and reliable Leopard for future deliveries. *(BD)*

Upper. One of four Leyland PD2 models with East Lancs bodies was number 881 (881 BTF). These were the last new rear-entrance-bodied double-deckers to join the Lancaster fleet. *(RM)*

Lower. East Lancs-bodied Leyland PD2 number 201 (201 YTE) was one of three supplied in 1963 which were Lancaster's first double-deckers with front entrances. Number 881 stands behind. *(STA)*

Above. Photographed in the City Centre in March 1973 is Seddon-bodied Leyland Leopard number 116 (NTD 116K), the first of six supplied in 1972, the body order having been transferred to Seddon following the fire at the works of East Lancashire Coachbuilders. *(RM)*

Below. Three examples of the Leyland National were purchased, the first arriving in December 1973 and the others in March 1974 just before the transfer of the undertaking to Lancaster City Transport. The model did not create a good impression and all three were sold to Fishwick of Leyland in March and April 1978. Number 124 (PTC 124M) was photographed in the City Centre on route 6 to Ridge Estate. *(BD)*

Above. The caption above the open topper on this commercial postcard reads *Come and Motor "Boat" on the Prom at Morecambe,* but where was the photographer standing, and is the driver trying to restart the engine? *(LCT)*

Below. One of the vehicles which passed to Morecambe and Heysham Corporation from Heysham and District on amalgamation was Karrier K1 TD 5314 which received fleet number 27. It is shown here in the red and white livery and operated until May 1935. *(JFH)*

Above. A maker's view of into Leyland G-type number L1 (TB 2557), taken when the bus was new and still carrying trade plates. Salford Corporation had a pair of almost identical vehicles delivered at this time. *(LCT)*

Below. Guy FBX G11 (TD 7300), with Short Brothers body dating from 1926, stands outside Morecambe Town Hall. The occasion is thought to be the introduction of the green livery. *(LCT)*

Upper. This Maudslay M3LBC with Northern Counties body dating from 1930 was claimed to be the country's only illuminated bus when it was decorated in this way in 1936. It was fitted with a generator to power the 757 coloured lamps. *(LCT)*

Middle. In 1932 six AEC Regents with Weymann bodies were purchased and began an association with AEC which was to remain until 1957. The bodies were built in Addlestone and number 30 (TF 7466) is illustrated here in service at Heysham. *(HPC)*

Lower. Typical of the Morecambe and Heysham pre-war fleet is number 17 (DTB 62), a Park Royal-bodied AEC Regent dating from 1938. (HPC)

Crowds gathered on the Promenade to view the scene after AEC Regent number 26 (BTF 237) toppled over into the sea shortly before the war. We wonder what the present day Health and Safety Executive would think of the improvised lifting equipment used to recover the vehicle. The lower photograph showing the vehicle after it had been raised indicated that the damage to the Park Royal body was not extensive and the bus was returned to service after repairs. *(LTC)*

Upper. The eleven Park Royal-bodied AEC Regents received in 1938 were the last new vehicles to be delivered until 1947. They were unusual in being fitted with petrol engines at a time when most operators were changing to diesel. Number 25 (DTB 64) is shown here in July 1959 when it was 21 years old, having received a diesel engine in October 1956. In the background is post-war Park Royal-bodied-AEC Regent III number 59 (KTF 588). *(RM)*

Lower. A return to Weymann was made for the bodies of the six AEC Regent IIIs supplied in 1951. They were numbered 73-78 and number 76 (MTE 638) was photographed on the Promenade in May 1962. *(RM)*

Above. Park Royal-bodied AEC Regent III number 67 (LTF 252) dating from 1950 is shown in the later livery incorporating more cream. *(RM)*

Below. Of the five Massey-bodied AEC Regent Vs supplied in 1957 number 84 ((793 ATD) was the only one to have platform doors as illustrated in this nearside view taken in July 1967. *(RM)*

Above. Travelling along the Promenade to Heysham Village in April 1970 is Park Royal-bodied AEC Regent III number 72 (MTC 540). When new it was displayed at the Commercial Motor Show at Earls Court in September 1950. *(RM)*

Below. After 28 years of purchasing AEC Regent double-deckers, the Department changed to Leyland for its 1960 deliveries which comprised three PD2/37 models with Massey bodies. They were numbered 87-89 and number 89 (35 MTD) is shown here. *(BD)*

Upper. A nostalgic scene at Morecambe's Euston Road Bus Station on a Saturday morning in August 1963. The scene is dominated by Ribble vehicles with some private coaches possibly on hire to Ribble or another major operator. The MCW Orion-bodied PD2 destined for Liverpool on service X31 would not provide the most comfortable of rides. In the background Corporation buses can be seen. There is no shortage of passengers. Those were the days. *(RIB)*

Lower. 1949 AEC Regent III number 60 (KTF 589) is shown on the Promenade after conversion to open top. *(KS)*

Upper. Morecambe's first single-deck vehicles for many years were six AEC Swifts with Pennine bodies numbered 1-6 and dating from 1967. Number 2 (CTJ 102E) is shown on the Promenade heading for Euston Road Station. *(KS)*

Middle. This view of number 5 (CTJ 105E) clearly shows the dual door arrangement provided on these buses. *(RM)*

Lower. Seddon RU number 15 (NTF 715M) with a Seddon body was one of two supplied in 1973 and fitted with high-back seating in an attempt to attract private hire customers. *(BD)*

Upper. Standing at the Battery, Morecambe on 29th March 1975 is number 881 (881 BTF), a former Lancaster Leyland PD2 with East Lancs body carrying 'City of Lancaster' fleetnames. *(BD)*

Lower. On the same day former Morecambe and Heysham Park Royal-bodied AEC Regent III number 79 (TTB 688) was photographed at Euston Road Bus Station, Morecambe with 'City of Lancaster' fleetnames on its Morecambe livery. *(BD)*

Upper. Former Lancaster East Lancs-bodied Leyland Leopard number 103 (103 UTF) dating from 1961 is shown entering Damside Street, Lancaster on 30th September 1976 carrying the blue and white livery. *(BD)*

Middle. Seddon-bodied Seddon RU number 11 (MTE 611K), stands at Euston Road Bus Station, Morecambe on 24th August 1974, displaying the 'City of Lancaster' fleetname on its former Morecambe and Heysham green and white livery. *(BD)*

Lower. Leyland National number 124 (PTC 124M) had received its blue and white livery when photographed entering Damside Street on 7th August 1976. *(BD)*

Upper. East Lancs-bodied Leyland PD2 number 204 (KTJ 204C) travels along Cable Street on 29th March 1975 carrying the 'City of Lancaster' fleetname on its Lancaster livery. *(BD)*

Lower. Photographed at the same spot, number 205 (KTJ 205C) of the same batch has already been painted into the new blue and white livery. *(BD)*

Upper. Former Morecambe and Heysham Massey-bodied Leyland PD2 number 87 (33 MTD) had also received the blue livery when photographed on Morecambe on 29th March 1975. *(BD)*

Lower. Displaying the 'City of Lancaster' fleetname on its Morecambe and Heysham green livery on 24th August 1974 is number 5 (CTJ 105E), a 1967 AEC Swift with Pennine body. *(BD)*

In 1979 Lancaster received five Leyland Leopards with Duple bodies. Three were 55-seat buses, of which number 151 (NCW 151T) is shown in the upper picture, travelling along Morecambe Promenade on its way to Heysham Village. *(BD)* The other two were coaches, one of which, number 12 (URN 12V) features below. *(MB)*

Two Atlanteans with coach-seated East Lancs bodies were purchased in 1983. These two pictures show number 222 (BFV 222Y) with the Lonsdale Coaches fleetname on the upper deck panels. *(TWWK)*

East Lancs-bodied Atlantean number 213 (WCK 213Y) turns on to the Promenade on its way to Overton on service 228.

D231 TBW was a Volkswagen LT55 with 25-seat body by Optare. New to Thames Transit in 1986 it was acquired in 1989 and originally numbered 231. Renumbered M5 in 1990 it is seen in this guise passing the premises of Waring and Gillow, the world famous furniture makers. *(HP)*

Dating from 1982 Alexander coach-bodied Leopard number 644 (WAO 644Y) came from Portsmouth Transit in 1991.

In 2005 Stagecoach painted 1981 East Lancs-bodied Atlantean number 204 (J204 HFR) in the former Morecambe and Heysham green livery. Now numbered 14204 it is shown working the park and ride service. *(RA)*

Upper. Former Fife Scottish Alexander-bodied Atlantean number 158 (NRG 158M) leaves Lancaster Bus Station for Heysham Towers on 8th April 1989. *(RM)*
Lower. East Lancs-bodied Leyland Atlantean number 207 ((URN 207V) is pictured in Euston Road, Morecambe on 4th April 1980 whilst operating on service 472 from Heysham Village to Lancaster University. *(BD)*

Above. A view of West End Parade, Morecambe, as a solitary tram makes its way towards Bare. There seems to be an abundance of landaus lined up awaiting passengers of which there would appear to be few. *(STA/KIT)*

Left. The Tramway Hotel sign in Lancaster provides a reminder of how things were in times past with a picture of tram number 7. *(MB)*

Right. The first post-war double-deckers in Lancaster were Crossley-bodied Crossleys arriving in 1947 and 1948. Number 965, shown in Lancaster Bus Station, was the last of the 1948 batch. *(STA/KIT)*

Above. Preserved Park Royal-bodied AEC Regent III, number 50 (JTE 546), displays the 'three cream bands' version of the Morecambe and Heysham livery as it travels along the Promenade heading for Heysham Village. *(STA)*

Below. Number 54 (KTF 583), another Park Royal-bodied Regent III, displays the later livery with a greater amount of cream as it awaits departure for Middleton Holiday Camp. *(HPC)*

Above. A posed photograph of East Lancs-bodied Leyland PD2 number 128 (128 DTD), one of four such vehicles delivered in 1957. Behind is an unidentified Leyland Panther, also bodied by East Lancs. *(STA)*

Below. Leyland Leopard L1, number 102 (102 UTF) with East Lancs body dating from 1961 is shown leaving Lancaster Bus Station for Ashfield Avenue. *(HPC)*

Above. Number 726 (FTD 726) was a Guy Arab which originally had a body by Pickering to wartime specification. It was rebodied in 1952 with a body built by Guy Motors on Park Royal frames. It is shown in the depot and in the background is number 47 (FTE 66), another Guy Arab which had been re-bodied in 1951 by Crossley Motors. *(HPC)*

Below. Number 80 (TTB 689) was an AEC Regent III with Park Royal lightweight body dating from 1954. It is shown on Morecambe Promenade on 19th September 1973 carrying the final Morecambe and Heysham double-deck livery prior to amalgamation with Lancaster. *(TWWK)*

Above. Number 203 (203 YTE) was one of three Leyland Titan PD2 models with East Lancs front entrance bodies delivered to Lancaster in 1963, that operators first front entrance double-deckers. *(HPC)*

Below. In 1957 Morecambe and Heysham made a change of body builder from Park Royal to Massey Brothers for five AEC Regent V chassis. One of these, number 85 (794 ATD), is heading along the Promenade towards Heysham Village. *(HPC)*

The scene outside Euston Road Bus Station, Morecambe on 10th July 1981 shows MCW-bodied Atlantean number 217 (DBA 217C), which had been new to Salford in 1965, crossing Euston Road to enter the Bus Station. In the lower picture East Lancs-bodied Atlantean number 209 (URN 209V), new in 1979, overtakes Ribble lowbridge Atlantean number 1806 as it heads for Overton. *(both HP)*

Heading out of Morecambe for Lancaster University on 10th July 1981, number 211 (DHG 211W) (above) displays the original version of the blue and white livery, whilst number 213 (WCK 213Y) (below), photographed in Garstang on 8th May 1987, shows the later version with light blue added. *(both HP)*

Morecambe and Heysham number 2 (CTJ 102E) was one of six AEC Swift rear-engined single-deckers with Pennine bodies supplied in 1967. It is pictured on the Promenade heading for Westgate on service 5. *(STA)* Number 58 (KTF 587), an AEC Regent III with Park Royal body, was new in 1949. It was converted to open–top in 1970 and is shown below in this form having received the 'City of Lancaster' fleetname following amalgamation. *(TWWK)*

Lancaster received three Leyland Nationals just prior to its amalgamation with Morecambe and Heysham, one of which, number 123 (PTC 123M) is pictured above. *(STA)* They had short lives with Lancaster and were the subject of a deal with J Fishwick and Sons of Leyland whereby two Leyland Leopard coaches with Plaxton bodies came to Lancaster. One of these, number 398 (VUB 398H) is shown below when operating on a Hornsea Pottery excursion in July 1978. *(MB)*

Number 389 (389 JTD), a Leyland Tiger Cub with East Lancs body new to Lancaster in 1959 emerges from North Road, Lancaster showing the latest blue and white livery. *(TWWK)*

Loading in Lancaster Bus Station in April 1979 is East Lancs-bodied Leopard number 113 (YTE 113H) dating from 1970. Behind is number 214, one of the MCW-bodied Atlanteans which had been new to Salford City Transport. *(MB)*

Travelling along Cable Street, having just left Lancaster Bus Station, is Leyland Leopard number 118 (NTD 118K) with Seddon body dating from 1972. The body order for these vehicles was originally with usual supplier East Lancashire Coachbuilders, but was transferred to Seddon because of a major fire at the manufacturer's works. *(TWWK)*

Heading along Morecambe Promenade on 10th July 1981 is East Lancs-bodied Leyland Leopard number 110 (RTE 110G) being overtaken by number 228 (DBA 228C), one of the Atlanteans new to Salford City Transport and which had been converted to open top. *(HP)*

Number 10 (UTJ 910H), an AEC Swift rear-engined single-decker with Northern Counties body, new in 1970 to Morecambe and Heysham, had received the blue and white livery when photographed on Morecambe Promenade. *(TWWK)*

Crossing Euston Road to the Bus Station on 10th July 1981 is Alexander-bodied Leyland Leopard number 309 (WCW 309R) which was new in 1977. *(HP)*

Two Leyland Atlanteans with coach-seated bodies by East Lancashire Coachbuilders were delivered in 1983 and numbered 221 and 222 (BFV 221/2Y). The upper photograph shows number 221 in fleet livery passing through Poulton le Fylde en route to Blackpool in September 1987. The lower photograph shows number 222 in Lancaster Bus Station in June 1983 displaying the special livery to mark 80 years of Transport in Lancaster. *(both MB)*

In the upper picture Atlantean number 212 (TCK 212X) shows the latest livery with upswept bands as it travels along Central Drive, Morecambe on service 228 to Overton on 13th August 1993. *(BD)*

Three front-engined Volvo Ailsa double-deckers with Northern Counties bodies were acquired from Greater Manchester Transport in 1990. One of these, 447 (WRJ 447X), is shown below at Lancaster Bus Station in August 1991 awaiting departure to Higher Heysham. *(MB)*

Upper

A scene in Kendal on 7th May 1988 as Alexander-bodied Leyland Leopard 316 (WCW 316R) leaves for Sandylands. *(BD)*

Middle

Indicative of private hire work undertaken is this view of Duple-bodied Leyland Tiger number 98 (D98 SCW) at Overstrand near Cromer on 24th June 1988. It was operating on a coach holiday to the Pleasaunce, Overstrand, for Christian Endeavour Holidays. *(HP)*

Lower

In the rural setting of Hornby, Alexander-bodied Leyland Leopard 318 (WCW 318R) operates the 0752 departure from Lancaster to Settle on 11th July 1989. *(BD)*

Upper

Shown at Heysham and displaying the latest single deck livery, Alexander-bodied Leyland Leopard number 312 (WCW 312R) operates the 1250 Lancaster to Combermere Road journey on 18th August 1993. *(BD)*

Middle

Heading along Blackhall Road, Kendal in the cream and blue dual-purpose livery is Alexander-bodied Leyland Leopard number 17 (MFR 17P). It is passing Ribble coach 1104 and is en route to Lancaster on service 6. *(HP)*

Lower

An unusual vehicle and an unusual scene for municipal operation. ECW-bodied Leyland Leopard number 827 (UKE 827X) climbs Buck Haw Brow on its journey from Settle to Lancaster on the last Saturday of operation, 21st August 1993. *(RA)*

LIFE AFTER LANCASTER

Upper

One of the Atlanteans taken over by Stagecoach was number 214 (A214 MCK) seen operating in Preston on 18th September 1993, now numbered 1214 but still in Lancaster livery. *(BD)*

Middle

A return to green. In the summer of 1997 Stagecoach introduced an open-top service between Heysham and Happy Mount Park using Olympian 2102 in Cumberland Lakeland livery. The vehicle is shown leaving Heysham Village on 18th July 1997. *(HP)*

Lower

Stagecoach painted Olympian 14204 in Morecambe and Heysham livery in 2005. Its first outing in these colours was for the Stagecoach Open Day and Rally at White Lund Depot, Morecambe on 28th May 2005 operating on a Park and Ride service. *(BD)*